LABYRINTH

SOLVING THE RIDDLE OF THE MAZE

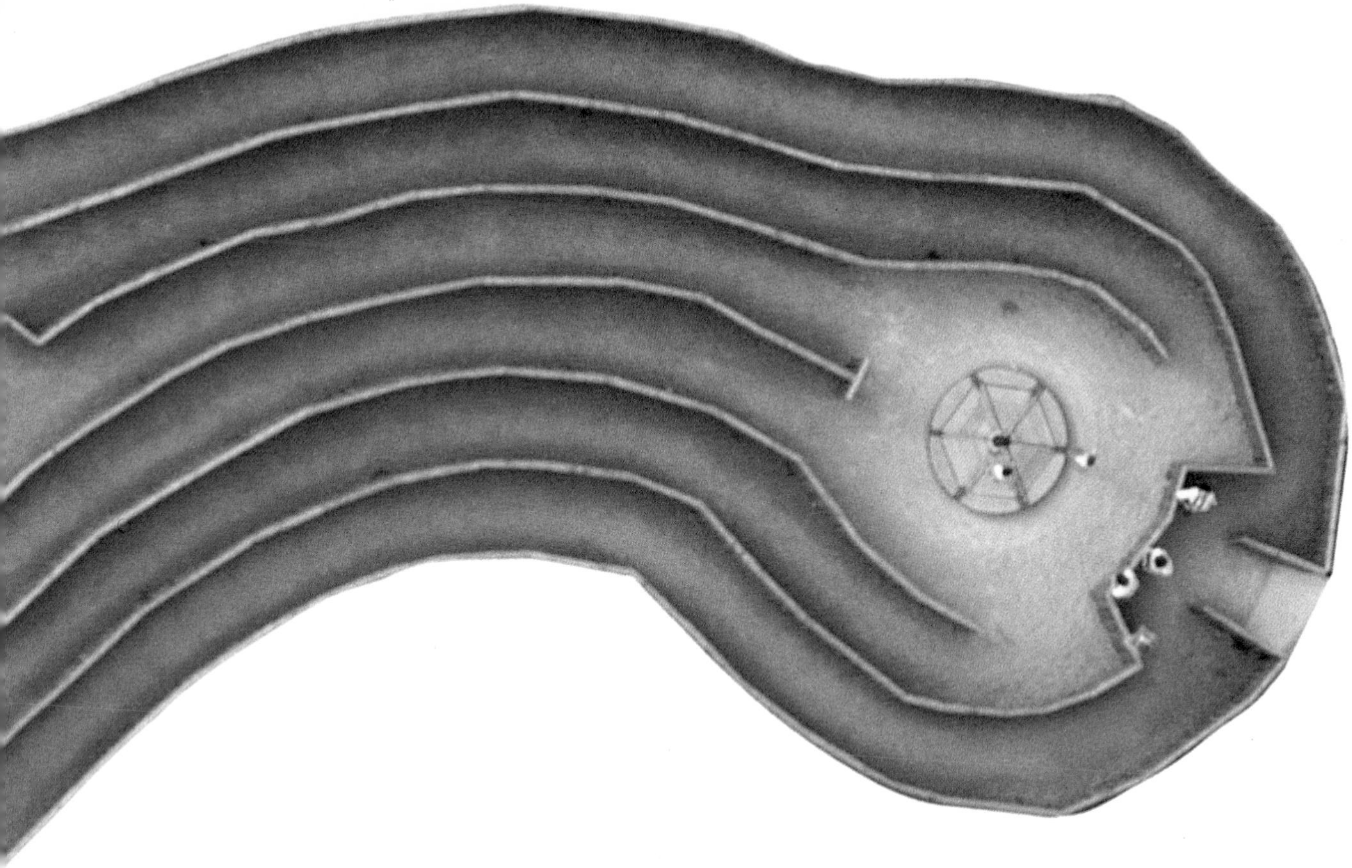

LABYRINTH

SOLVING THE RIDDLE OF THE MAZE

Adrian Fisher & Georg Gerster

HARMONY BOOKS
a division of Crown Publishers, Inc.
New York

Published by Harmony Books, a division of Crown Publishers, Inc., 201 East 50th Street, New York 10022. Member of the Crown Publishing Group.

Originally published in Great Britain by George Weidenfeld and Nicolson Ltd in 1990

Manufactured in Italy

Library of Congress Cataloguing-in-Publication Data

Fisher, Adrian.
Labryinth: solving the riddle of the maze/by Adrian Fisher. —
1st ed.
p. cm.
1. Maze gardens. I. Title.
SB475.F57 1990
712—dc20
90-36614
CIP
ISBN 0-517-58099-3
10 9 8 7 6 5 4 3 2 1

First American Edition

pages 2–3 The Bicton maze
pages 4–5 Hever Castle Maze

Contents

Acknowledgements

To each new maze owner, who has participated in the act of creation and made possible the development of this unusual art – this book is their gallery.

To Jane, Felicity and Katharine Fisher for all their patience and support; Randoll Coate, fellow explorer of so many maze design adventures, for his friendship and wit; Pammy and Marion Coate for their good-humoured encouragement; Lesley Beck for her design talent, and practical approach to maze construction; Georg Gerster, who introduced me to the Daedalean art of aerial photography; Jeff and Debbie Saward for founding the Caerdroia Project, and for their superb research material, sustained encouragement and unstinting help; John Kraft, for his prolific and meticulous research both in Scandinavia and further afield; Nigel Pennick, for his enthusiastic research; Anthony Camacho and Edward Hordern, fellow adventurers in colour maze design; the late Dudley Heesom, for his perceptive early encouragement; Zeta Eastes, daughter of W. H. Matthews, for her infectious enthusiasm; Barbara Cheales for her kindness; my parents for their encouragement, and my mother for her energetic needlework; Linden Gray and Jacquie McNulty for their help in North America; Graham Burgess for his help in the past; Phil Collins for all his advice; and William Fisher, Nick and Stephanie Evans, Tielmann Nicolopoulos, Diana Kingham, Ian Powys, Terry Lockyer and Christine Ainger for their help and support. A.F.

I shall be forever grateful to Greg Bright, for having instilled into me the joy of running mazes; to the late Hermann Kern, for giving me food for thought on them; to John Kraft, for inciting me to see them in a context of tradition and culture; to Stuart Landsborough, for teaching me the mechanics of designing them; and to Adrian Fisher, maze-maker supreme, for feeding my labyrinthomania with ever more intriguing creations. G.G.

PICTURE ACKNOWLEDGEMENTS

B. & C. Alexander p 47 bottom, p 49, p 85, p 95
Janet and Colin Bord p 13, p 26 bottom, p 27 bottom right, p 31 left, p 31 top, p 31 bottom, p 45
Trustees of the British Museum p 16
Paul Broadhurst/Janet and Colin Bord p 13
Caerdroia, Chris Castle p 150
Caerdroia, John Kraft p 23 top
Caerdroia, Jeff Saward p 17, p 18, p 27 bottom, p 28, p 30 top, p 31 right, p 32, p 38 left, p 39, p 40 right, p 44, p 68, p 131 top, p 136, p 137, p 141, p 151
The Earl of Cawdor p 87 top
The Royal Library of Copenhagen p 50 top
Adrian Fisher p 20, p 41, p 42 right, p 43, p 49 top, p 50 bottom, p 60–1, p 63 right, p 64, p 65, p 66 left, p 67 bottom, p 69, p 71, p 73, p 74, p 75 bottom, p 77, p 84, p 87 bottom, p 89 bottom, p 90–1, p 93 bottom, p 98, p 102, p 104 bottom, p 105, p 106 bottom, p 107 bottom, p 108, p 110, p 112, p 114 left, p 115 right, p 116, p 117 p 122, p 124, p 125, p 126, p 127, p 131 top, p 131 bottom, p 132, p 133, p 134, p 135, p 143
Fortean Picture Library p 51 top, p 52, p 53 top, p 100, p 144
Georg Gerster p 10, p 14, p 21, p 22, p 29, p 46, p 47 top, p 54, p 56, p 59, p 62, p 70, p 72, p 78, p 80, p 86, p 88, p 89, p 92, p 94, p 96–7, p 99, p 101, p 103, p 104 top, p 111, p 113, p 114 right, p 115 left, p 118, p 119, p 120, p 121, p 123, p 126, p 128–9, p 139, p 146, p 147, p 148, p 149
Guildhall Library, London p 82
By permission of the Dean and Chapter of Hereford Photo: Gordon W. Taylor p 38 right
A. W. kancken, Kalkmålningarna, Sibbo gamla kyrka, Finkst Museum, Vol 42, 1935, p 29, Helsingtors 1936 p 23 below
From Hermann Kern (*see Further Reading*), p 12 (Rainer Pauli, Dorfen), p 26, p 35 (Soprintendenza alle antichità della Lombardia, Milano), p 63 left
Kunsthistorisches Museum, Vienna p 34
The Mansell Collection p 30 centre, p 40 left, p 42 left, p 66 top, p 67 top
Museo Nazionale Athens p 27 top
Millar and Harris p 75 top
Diputacion Foral de Navarra, Museo de Navarra, Pamplona p 33
By kind permission of HM the Queen p 51 bottom
Rolawn p 138
By courtesy of the Trustees of Sir John Soane's Museum p 93 top
Staatliche Museen Preussischer Kulturbesitz, Kunstbibliothek, Berlin p 53 bottom, p 145
Uttlesford District Council p 140
Weidenfeld and Nicolson archives p 106 left, p 107 top, p 109 (George Wright)
Woburn Abbey Collection: by kind permission of the Marquess of Tavistock, and the Trustees of the Bedford Estates p 83

The publishers have taken all possible care to trace and acknowledge the source of illustrations. If any errors have accidentally occurred, the publishers will be happy to correct them in future editions, provided they receive notification.

Blenheim Palace.

Mazes have an extraordinary presence. Once seen, a maze cannot be ignored. It draws you into it like a magnet, then proceeds to puzzle, infuriate and delight in turn until its goal is reached. Mazes have been exerting this maddening fascination for thousands of years, and evidence of them is to be found in different civilisations all over the world.

Among the most famous is the yew maze at Hampton Court Palace which has been losing people between its tall hedges for some three hundred years. Here at Blenheim Palace we have now created the world's largest symbolic hedge maze, a fitting tribute to the heritage of which it has become a part, and an exciting addition to the oeuvre of one of the most vibrant of contemporary art forms.

What is the attraction of mazes, and why have they endured and re-created themselves, phoenix-like, from century to century in all parts of the world? This book offers an insight into the history, evolution and art of the maze, and reveals the sheer delight that is to be found in mazes while following the labyrinthine way.

Marlborough

Glossary of Maze Terms

ADJUSTABLE MAZE A maze whose barriers can be adjusted from day to day, or session to session. During any period when visitors are actually exploring the maze, the design remains static.

ANGLE-TYPE LABYRINTH DESIGN Strictly not a term to be encouraged, but used by Scandinavian labyrinth researchers (John Kraft and others) for all Classical unicursal labyrinths, with 3, 7, 11, 15, etc. rings of paths. Probably clearer to keep to the term CLASSICAL LABYRINTH DESIGN.

BLACK HOLE A maze situation which one can get into, but not get out of. Can occur in COLOUR MAZES. The opposite of a WHITE HOLE.

CAERDROIA Welsh word, usually for a unicursal turf labyrinth.

CENTRE Another word for GOAL, usually when the goal is reasonably central or symmetrically placed. Some pavement mazes and manuscript mazes have images of a Minotaur or of a Centaur at their centre, both taurean by name, both unnatural hybrid creatures. There is scant evidence that centre is a corruption of Centaur.

CLASSICAL LABYRINTH DESIGN The archetypal design, found in many parts of the world. Often but not always with seven rings of paths. All changes of path direction occur on the central axis between the entrance and the goal. Also known as ANGLE-TYPE, and CRETAN.

CLEW A ball of thread. Ariadne's ball of golden thread was the vital 'clue' that helped Theseus overcome the Minotaur within the labyrinth. There is little evidence that clue and clew are related, other than by their pronunciation in the English language.

CONDITIONAL DIRECTION MAZE A maze with one-way passages.

CONDITIONAL MOVEMENT MAZE A maze where each move depends on the previous move. The choice at each junction depends on how you approach it. A COLOUR MAZE is an example of a conditional movement maze.

COLOUR MAZE A maze where path colour is a crucial part of the puzzle. Contrasts with all other mazes, which are monochrome.

CRETAN LABYRINTH DESIGN Not a term to be encouraged. The term arose after ancient Cretan coins were found showing Classical seven-ring labyrinth designs, both circular and square. It is clearer to use the term CLASSICAL LABYRINTH DESIGN.

DEAD END Also known as a STOP.

DOOLHOF Dutch word, usually for a puzzle hedge maze.

ENTRANCE Every maze must have one, and some have more than one.

FORCED PATH A maze situation which only has one way forward. Encountered in COLOUR MAZES.

FRYING PAN A feature within a THREE-DIMENSIONAL MAZE, whereby the perimeter of an area cannot be penetrated. The way out is by a bridge over the perimeter, or through a tunnel under it.

GOAL The objective of the maze. Nearly all mazes have a goal, and usually only one.

HAND-ON-WALL METHOD A method which solves SIMPLY-CONNECTED mazes, but is defeated by MULTIPLY-CONNECTED mazes.

INTERACTIVE MAZE A maze whose design changes in response to actions of visitors.

INTERNAL ROTATIONAL SYMMETRY A hallmark of all Classical, Roman and medieval Christian labyrinths. If the design is cut from the entrance to the goal and 'folded out' to form a rectangle, then the resulting array of parallel paths should possess rotational symmetry.

IRRGARTEN German word, usually for a puzzle hedge maze.

ISLAND A continuously linked piece of hedging (or other barrier) within a maze, not linked to the perimeter hedge. Islands only occur in multicursal mazes.

LABYRINTH From the original Greek word, and adopted in most languages. Thought to be derived from *Labrys*, the double axe, sign of Zeus and symbol of Minoan power. Although interchangeable with maze, labyrinth tends to apply to mineral, and maze to vegetal networks.

MARKERS Leaving markers about in a maze to record one's progress is considered very bad form. Fortunately, if others are present in the maze, the spirit of Iitoi is likely to move your markers about.

MAZE Usually associated with English hedge mazes, but loosely used in the English speaking world for all kinds of labyrinths or labyrinthine situations.

MEDIEVAL CHRISTIAN DESIGN Unicursal maze design, with paths doubling back on all four axes, thus producing a cruciform image. The most common number of rings of paths is eleven, although seven and fifteen are also found. Also loosely referred to as the Chartres-type design.

MONOCHROME MAZES All kinds of maze where path colour is not significant. Contrasts with COLOUR MAZES, where path colour is central to their puzzlement.

MULTIPLY-CONNECTED A multicursal maze with forking paths, some of which link up with each other further on in the maze; thus it will have one or more islands within it. A multiply-connected maze must have its GOAL located on an ISLAND.

NODE A junction or decision-point, where three or more paths meet.

NOTATION Graph Theory, the study of networks, offers a form of notation for the most complex of mazes. Any maze can be represented by a matrix. This form of analysis can be applied to complex mazes which are not readily solvable by sight.

PAVEMENT A maze or labyrinth where the paths and barriers are both at the same height, and are only distinguished by the colour or texture of their materials.

PROCESSIONAL LABYRINTH Very similar to a UNICURSAL labyrinth, but with an additional short exit from the goal. This makes it possible for a procession of infinite length to pass through the maze without congestion at the goal.

QUICK EXIT In a puzzle maze, a quick exit avoids doubling the time of the visit, after reaching the goal. If the maze is multiply-connected, this can only be preserved if the quick exit crosses over or under the perimeter path, by bridge or tunnel.

RIB A segment of one ring of path between two axes of a labyrinth, usually unicursal. In a medieval Christian labyrinth, there are four ribs per ring of path, and a total of forty-four ribs.

RING One or more strips of path equidistant from the centre of a labyrinth, which together encompass the centre by nearly 360°. There are eleven rings in a medieval Christian labyrinth.

SIMPLY-CONNECTED A multicursal maze with a series of dead-ends leading off the one true path. Although one or more islands may be present, the goal is attached albeit tenuously to the perimeter.

SPAN A unit of measure, for comparison between mazes of different scales. In a barrier maze, a span is measured from the centre-line of one barrier to the centre-line of the next. In a turf or pavement maze, a span may be measured from the centre-line of one path to the centre-line of the next.

SPAN-SQUARE An imaginary square measured along the length of a path, based on the maze's span unit. The number of span squares containing nodes can be expressed as a percentage of the total number of span squares in the maze. This is one useful way to evaluate the difficulty of a maze.

STRAIGHT-LINE DIAGRAM A way of summarizing the topology of a maze, whilst eliminating non-essential detail. The entrance, a triangle, is connected to the goal, a circle, by the shortest solution, a straight line. Incidental paths fork off each side of the line.

THREE-DIMENSIONAL MAZE A maze whose paths cross over and under each other.

TIME-DIMENSIONAL MAZE A maze whose barriers can change from moment to moment whilst visitors are inside it. Time provides an extra dimension, but only forwards.

UNICURSAL 'Single-pathed', a maze with no junctions or decision points (NODES). From the GOAL, the visitor has to retrace his path entirely to return to the entrance.

WHIRLPOOL A harmless eddy within a maze, which one can get into and out of without difficulty. Can occur in COLOUR MAZES.

WHITE HOLE A maze situation which one cannot get into, but if one was in it, one could get out of it. Can occur in COLOUR MAZES. The oposite of a BLACK HOLE.

Origins and History

Daedalus designed it
King Minos built it
Asterion the Minotaur guarded it
Ariadne unravelled it
Theseus solved it
Thera destroyed it
Arthur Evans couldn't find it

THE RIDDLE OF the maze reaches back several millennia, and is spread over many parts of the world. Great distances and hazardous travel separated early civilizations, and their relative isolation produced a great diversity of alphabets, languages and dialects. Yet, remarkably, one archetypal labyrinth design prevailed throughout the world for thousands of years.

The earliest rock carvings were cup and ring marks, spirals, and the complete infilling of spiralled grooves and ridges. These early rock carvings hint at a preoccupation with the inner spirit and the journey through life to death. The earliest labyrinth designs probably evolved from spirals, when man started devising geometric constructions. Rock carvings of the identical seven-ring labyrinthine design have been found at Luzzanas in Sardinia (*c.* 2500–2000 BC, or possibly later), Padugula in South India (*c.* 1000 BC), Val Camonica in Northern Italy (*c.* 750–550 BC) and Kom Ombo in Egypt (*c.* 30 BC).

PREVIOUS PAGE *The turf maze at Tibble follows the Classical labyrinth design. Set in a grove of trees it conjures all the mystery of ancient rites hinted at by Tacitus.*

The rock carving at Luzzanas in Sardinia, possibly the world's oldest surviving labyrinth.

The maze at Rocky Valley, Tintagel, Cornwall, is carved according to the Classical labyrinth design.

The same seven-ring design appears on coins from Knossos in the British Museum collection (*c.* 430–67 BC). In Sutan in East Afghanistan, a seven-ring labyrinth drawing portrays 'Shamaili's House', which only the Princess Shamaili knew how to enter. In India, the temple of Halebid in Mysore has a seven-ring labyrinth carved within a twelfth- or thirteenth-century stone frieze. In Arizona, the labyrinth carvings at Casa Grande and Oraibi date back to the thirteenth century, or perhaps slightly later. In the Rocky Valley near Tintagel in Cornwall, the same seven-ring design is found carved on a vertical rock face. In Scandinavia, there are at least 530 Classical labyrinths made from rings of stones or boulders, some possibly dating back over a thousand years. In Iceland, a stone labyrinth known as Volundarhus (Wayland's House) is one of four labyrinths dating from sometime after the eleventh century. In Sumatra, labyrinths have been found carved on timbers of houses and the gold finger-rings of remote jungle tribes.

Traces of labyrinthine patterns in earthworks and pictorial art reach back into prehistory. Some earthworks had a symbolic or spiritual meaning, although the great majority were erected for defence. The earliest surviving forms of art are cave paintings and rock carvings. These depict not only practical hunting scenes, but also abstract spirals and patterns.

It would seem that labyrinths possibly sprang up in different parts of the world independently of each other. Although the idea seems attractive, there is no evidence that Cretan coins, through sea trade, disseminated the labyrinth design throughout the ancient known world. However, once mastered, the method of construction of the Classical seven-ring labyrinth is so easily memorized that there would have been no need to record it, so knowledge of it could have travelled with seafarers across great distances. It may have had an inherent mathematical fascination, rather like the right-angled triangle in the ratio 3:4:5 or the knowledge of the reef knot. Whilst retaining its design integrity, its cultural significance may have become lost or confused, and then adopted by another culture and given new meanings.

Different cultures and traditions have separate myths, which are not descended from one another, yet the ancient Classical seven-ring labyrinth seems universal: seven rings of paths, contained within eight concentric walls.

The earliest origins of the maze are buried beneath the sands of time, but myths and legends emerge from the mist, tantalizing us with their ideas, and teasing us with their ambiguous nature. The word labyrinth is possibly derived from *labrys*, the ritual double-headed axe of the Minoan civilization on Crete. The labrys was used extensively in their worship, and as part of the cult of the bull, whose two horns it imitates. Maze patterns found on the walls of the palace of Knossos also have the appearance of a double-headed axe.

The Palace at Knossos may have housed the Minotaur in one part of it.

The best-known labyrinth myth is the Greek story of Theseus slaying the Minotaur. Other traditions have no such monstrous creature. Instead, the

labyrinth is a walled city or fortification which only the cogniscenti can enter, the womb-like bower of a maiden or goddess, or a place of retreat and protection for its initiates. Indeed, the labyrinth has been a place of initiation by ritual procession, from childhood into adulthood. The labyrinth also has powerful sexual imagery, with the seed entering and penetrating, and the life of the newborn child emerging. There are clear parallels with the concept of reincarnation. The labyrinth has also been used to draw upon spiritual or magical powers, such as prosperity and fertility, personal safety on a voyage, or control of the weather.

There are several variations to the legend of Theseus and the Minotaur, but the main story is clear. Crete had won a victory over Athens, and as a cruel tribute, required that every nine years, seven young men and seven maidens should be sent to Crete, to be devoured by the Minotaur in a labyrinth. The fourteen victims were chosen by lot, bringing terror to every family in Athens whenever the tribute became due. Finally Theseus, son of King Aegeus, volunteered to join the ship, determined to resolve the matter by killing the Minotaur. If Theseus survived, it was agreed that the ship would return with a white sail, otherwise it would hoist a black one.

Theseus and his party were approaching a most unusual island. Queen Paisiphae, sexually unsatisfied by King Minos, had ordered the talented inventor Daedalus to construct a convincing full-size model of a cow, in which she could conceal herself. Zeus, greatest of the gods, descended in the form of a bull and impregnated her. The result was the birth of the Minotaur, half man, half beast. Daedalus was a talented inventor, and is attributed with the invention of carpentry tools, the lost-wax process of casting metal and much more. Now he was required to build a labyrinth, in which to contain the Minotaur. It was clearly most effective, since the Minotaur never escaped, and according to the myth none of the Athenian men and maidens who preceded Theseus had ever survived after entering it.

Theseus and his companions duly arrived on Crete and Theseus somehow persuaded the King's daughter Ariadne, who knew the one weakness of the Cretan labyrinth, to help him. She provided him with a ball of golden thread, and told him precisely how to use it. Theseus then entered the labyrinth, slew the Minotaur, and thus broke the cruel tribute. Finally, the survivors sailed towards Athens, inexplicably returning under a black sail. In grief King Aegeus threw himself off a cliff into the sea which still bears his name, and Theseus immediately became the new King of Athens.

In his turn, Daedalus also wanted to leave Crete, but King Minos forbade him. Undaunted, Daedalus made two pairs of wings held together with wax, to help him and his son Icarus to escape. On their way, Icarus flew too near the sun, the wax melted, and he plunged to his death into the sea. Daedalus safely completed his flight, but the price was the life of his only son.

The Cretan labyrinth myth offers numerous tempting alleyways to explore and there are many possible interpretations. The entry by Theseus into the labyrinth possibly did not take place at the planned time for the ritual, when there may have been armed guards forcing the fourteen victims into the labyrinth and on the look-out for trouble. If Theseus had waited until that time, he would have risked confiscation of the vital ball of golden thread and any concealed weapon.

It is possible, therefore, that Theseus made a pre-emptive move to slay the Minotaur. Certainly he was able to escape from Crete with all his companions, taking Ariadne with him against her father's will. On their way home, they landed on the island of Naxos, and performed a crane dance. Theseus then abandoned Ariadne on the island, either because the passion of one or both had cooled, or because Ariadne had served her purpose as a hostage, and continued his journey home without her.

There are few clues within the myth as to the nature of the Cretan labyrinth. Cretan coins of the third century BC had labyrinths on them, of the Classical seven-ring design. However, this design has no junctions and only smooth paths and walls, so it is difficult to understand why a golden thread should have been needed. We can only assume that this seven-ring design was a convenient emblem to encapsulate the essence of the situation, yet obviously a gross simplification that would need no explanation to contemporary eyes. We use this every day ourselves – consider the range of international road signs, whose purpose is to convey a vital image in a fraction of a second, with impact and conciseness being more important than literal accuracy. Perhaps the labyrinth was dark inside, so the golden thread could give Theseus guidance, especially if the paths between the walls were too wide to touch both sides at once. In the darkness, the gold may have reflected any faint light, and behaved as if it were luminous.

Apparently the Cretan labyrinth was intricate and extensive, and might have had junctions giving an element of choice. The junctions could have been created by many parallel rows of pillars, as in the great Egyptian labyrinth at Fayum. Alternatively, the labyrinth may have been an extensive area of interconnecting rooms within the palace, to contain the monstrous royal offspring. Arthur Evans' reconstruction of part of the Palace of Knossos creates just this kind of atmosphere, with a three-dimensional effect produced by open-well staircases.

If the labyrinth contained junctions and dead ends, it could prove fatal to become trapped in one of these, rendering one vulnerable to being gored to death by the Minotaur. A golden thread would have kept Theseus to the one true path each time he needed to retreat. His method of attack may have been to approach the Minotaur unseen, leap into view, make one bloody lunge at the creature, and then retreat rapidly along the line of the golden thread until

OPPOSITE LEFT *Coins from Crete in the British Museum collection, showing their distinctive square or circular 'Classical' labyrinth pattern. They date from 430 to 67* BC.

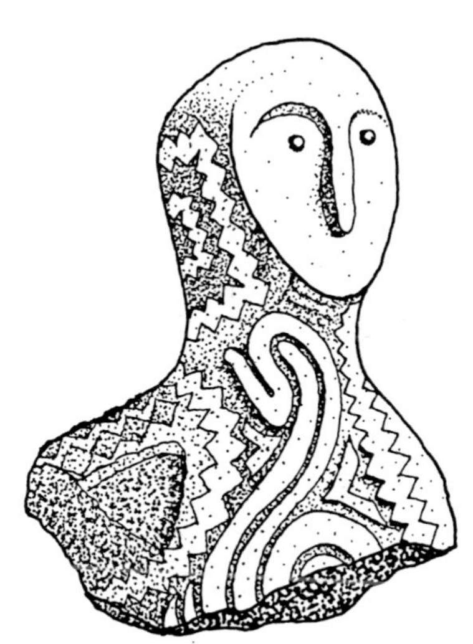

Figurine of a bird-cum-snake goddess found at Vadastra, Romania, dating to c. 4500 BC. *The crane dance may have originated from the worship of the Crane goddess in the Danube delta.*

hidden within the labyrinth. After a few minutes of Minotaurean rage, the beast would have settled down to lick the wound, and then Theseus could have crept up again and inflicted the next stab. The Minotaur would thus have died a death of a thousand cuts, not unlike present-day bull-fighting. The labyrinth itself, or part of it, may have been like a bull-fighting arena, with inner walls to jump over or retreat behind, where the alley would be too narrow for the bull to follow.

The labyrinth could have been underground, perpetually in darkness. It may have been constructed like a medieval oubliette, with the only entrance a vertical hole downwards to the cell below. Such an entrance would have prevented the Minotaur (and anyone else) from escaping. The golden thread may therefore have been a strong rope, used to climb back upwards through this hole, although this suggestion does not reconcile with the notion of a hand-held ball of golden twine, providing guidance rather than physical strength.

This myth even provides clues that the labyrinth symbol is far older than the Cretan labyrinth itself. Theseus, Ariadne and their companions performed the 'Geranos', a crane dance, on the island of Naxos. This ancient dance is performed by a line of people, possibly consisting of nine steps and a hop, in imitation of the action of the crane bird. The Crane goddess was worshipped in the eastern Mediterranean and the Danube delta between 6500 and 3500 BC. Many figurines of bird goddesses have been found, inscribed with meander patterns which have a close connection with formal labyrinth designs.

On a symbolic level, the Cretan labyrinth with its golden thread portrays the cycle of life, by representing the womb and the umbilical cord. The male seed enters and explores the dark and secret passages, until he successfully penetrates and transforms the inner half-completed life-form; the umbilical cord is vital to his safe exit from the womb. For Theseus, the crane dance was part of his ritual initiation into adulthood, before he went out into the world to accomplish his life's work, and gain his kingdom.

The creation myth of the Tohono O'otam (formerly known as the Papago) and Pima tribes of Southern Arizona can take up to four days to tell in words and song. It is called the House of Iitoi and this simplified version (formulated by Jeff Saward) emphasizes the key point of the labyrinth connection.

A labyrinth from a manuscript, the Rudo Ensayo, *of* c. *1762, said to show the plan of a building by a Piman Indian.*

'In the beginning, ... there was only darkness, inhabited by Earthmaker and Buzzard. Earthmaker rubbed dirt from his skin and held it in his hand, from which grew the greasewood bush. With a ball of gum taken from this bush, Earthmaker created the world. As Buzzard created the mountains and rivers with the passage of its wings, the Spider People sewed the earth and the sky together.

'In time, Earthmaker brought about a race of people in the desert. These people lived for several generations, but as time went on they became sinful, all except one, Iitoi, the Elder Brother (called Se'eh ha by the Pima). Earthmaker saw that Iitoi was true and told him that a flood would soon kill all the people in the desert. The Creator placed Iitoi high up on the sacred mountain Baboquivari and let him witness the disaster.

'Afterwards Iitoi helped create the Hohokam from whom the Tohono O'otam and the Pima people descended. He helped teach them the right way in life, and they lived in harmony for many years. However in time eventually some of the people turned upon Iitoi and killed him . . . his spirit fled back atop Baboquivari, where it remains to this day.

'From time to time Iitoi's spirit, in the form of a very small man, would cunningly sneak into the villages and take things from the people. In their attempts to catch him they would get confused at all the deceiving turns he made returning to his home atop the peak. Thus in the maze one can see Iitoi on the pathway and trace his mysterious and bewildering turns on the journey back to Baboquivari . . . his mountain home.'

There are remarkable parallels with the Christian Old and New Testaments, with Creation, the Fall, the Flood, unjust Execution, Resurrection and Ascension. Iitoi is both Noah escaping the Flood on a sacred mountain, and also the sinless Christ, the teacher of the right way of life, who dies at the hands of evil people, and then appears in a resurrected human form. Even his method of departure has parallels with Christ's Ascension, using a labyrinth to distance himself from his followers, every bit as effective as Christ going up in a cloud.

The Classical seven-ring labyrinth design is known as the House of Iitoi, or *Se'eh ha Ki* in the Piman language. Although the Arizona labyrinths contain the Classical seven rings of paths, there are three notable differences, which suggest that the labyrinth tradition in Arizona is original. Firstly, the arms of the barriers all approach the centre. This significant departure is characteristic of Arizonan labyrinths, including the designs on modern basketwork and jewellery, and is not found anywhere else in the world. Secondly, Arizonan labyrinths are portrayed with their entrance at the top, whilst most Classical labyrinths are portrayed with their entrance beneath.

Thirdly, the design is always shown with the Elder Brother, the man in the maze. No other labyrinth tradition consistently portrays a male figure. The male Iitoi, the Elder Brother, is at the entrance of the labyrinth, about to enter, but never inside it. There is no female involved in Iitoi's story. The perfect and celibate Iitoi has his counterpart with the labyrinth, rather like Christ who referred to the church as His Bride.

At one level, the labyrinth symbolizes the female womb, only penetrable if

Basketwork from Arizona showing the Man in the Maze.

one is pure and perfect. The male figure outside, representing the human seed, can penetrate the womb, fertilize the ovum, produce new life, which then emerges as a new birth or a reincarnated existence. Entry into the labyrinth gives new life to Iitoi, thus achieving reincarnation and eternal life.

The Tohono O'otam still consider the House of Iitoi design as a symbol of individual, family and tribal birth. Iitoi's progress through the labyrinth represents the many turns and changes of life, as he acquires knowledge and understanding. The centre of the labyrinth represents approaching death, but Iitoi bypasses this to the end of the pathway, where he can reflect upon his life and finally accept his death.

Other explanations for the labyrinth tradition of the south-western states of America have been given from the point of view of European settlers. Several labyrinth carvings have been found near Jesuit missions, and it is often suggested that the design was introduced by missionaries accompanying Spanish expeditions in the late seventeenth century. A priest Eusebio Kino visited and celebrated mass at Casa Grande in 1694, and was the first to describe the ruins.

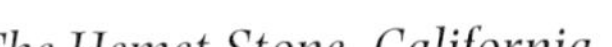

The Hemet Stone, California.

The theory of a recent European introduction is, however, seriously flawed, since several of the labyrinths in the south-west can be dated earlier than the sixteenth century. For example, a labyrinth carving at Casa Grande, Arizona, was scratched into wet plaster on the inner wall of a building. If, as seems likely, it is contemporary with the building, it was probably made between AD 1100 and 1200, and certainly earlier than AD 1450 when Casa Grande was abandoned. Subsequently the carving was concealed by undisturbed rubble, and only excavated by archaeologists in 1906–8.

It is difficult to comprehend why Indians should be interested in a European myth, let alone embed it deeply into their ancient and sacred oral tradition. The Jesuits had come to preach Christianity, so it seems astonishing that they would bring a pre-Christian design, when the medieval Christian design was already available. Nor is there any evidence of a Christian labyrinth tradition in Spain at that time. The correlation between labyrinths and Jesuit missions in Arizona can be simply explained, since the Jesuits would naturally have built their missions near existing tribal settlements, which already possessed labyrinths.

Several labyrinths in Finland and Sweden are named *Jungfrudanser*, meaning virgin dances. These were performed entirely by young people, and were kept secret from parents and older folk.

In one of these dances, a virgin stood at the centre, and others formed a procession and danced towards her along the paths of the labyrinth. In another, a young man would run through the labyrinth, and then dance with the girl at the centre. In another variation, a boy would try to reach the girl and then carry her out of the labyrinth; if he did this without making any mistakes, the girl was his. The dancing was sustained by spectators singing and clapping their hands, and special objects such as horseshoes were placed along the paths, for good luck. The suggestion that these dances and races were part of the universal ritual of boy pairing with girl is reinforced by various items of clothing having different meanings, which could affect the future happiness of the couple. In another version of the story the labyrinth was a fortified prison, and the young man had to weave his way to the girl, in order to liberate her.

All these dances share the common idea of placing a girl or virgin at the centre, with the male role being to run through the labyrinth to reach her. The finding and rescuing of a maiden in a fortress prison is the inspiration of children's fairy tales in many countries.

Interestingly, the female figure is placed at the centre of Scandinavian labyrinths, in contrast to the male portrayed at the entrance of labyrinths in Arizona. Moreover, the latter are all portrayed the opposite way up. Effectively, all Scandinavian labyrinths are portrayed from the point of view of the man, about to run into the labyrinth towards the woman.

Many labyrinths in northern Europe bear the names of famous cities. The names of Troy, Babylon, Nineveh, Jericho, Jerusalem and Constantinople reach back into antiquity, whilst medieval Nordic cities such as Trondheim and Viborg have also provided names for labyrinths.

Troy and Jericho suffered two of the great sieges of ancient times. Both labyrinths and cities are manifestations of permanent settlement, and the antithesis of hunter-gathering or the nomadic way of life. These two cities had seemingly impregnable walls, which only yielded by deception or supernatural power. The walls of Jericho 'yielded' after a ritual procession involving seven circuits – precisely what is needed to make a seven-ring Classical labyrinth yield to an individual or procession. In the bible, an earthquake caused the walls to yield to the Israelites, with the miracle being both the timing and the precision of the power.

The city of Troy had withstood siege from its Greek enemies for several years. Helen, the requisite female within the maze waiting to be rescued, was held hostage within Troy. As at Jericho, the overcoming of the walls involved their partial destruction, in this case by the greed of the Trojans, who were so

The 'Jungfruringen' or Virgin Ring at Kopmanholm north east of Stockholm had two entrances. Two boys raced in opposite directions to try to reach the girl first.

Fifteenth-century wall-painting from the old church in Sibbo, Nyland, Finland, showing a virgin at the centre of the labyrinth.

LEFT OPPOSITE *Stone labyrinth on the significantly-named Jungfrau Island in Sweden, meaning Virgin Island. The fundamental method of construction is the same as in seven-ring Classical labyrinths.*

keen to bring the wooden horse within the city. The wooden horse is itself an object of great curiosity – a fantastic creature, comparable with the mythical Minotaur, employing the art of deception to penetrate the ultimate walls of deception. As with the Cretan labyrinth, the intruder prevails. Indeed, the exploitation of an inherent weakness lies at the heart of many Greek myths, from Achilles' heel to Ariadne's thread.

The Romans had a similar idea of labyrinths. They portrayed them as forts, with battlements and towers. Their labyrinths were usually square, which was also the preferred shape of Roman forts and fortified cities, and the shape of most Roman mosaic pavement mazes.

Indian labyrinth designs are often called *Kote*, which means fort. A labyrinth illustrates the castle of the demon Ravana in the Indian epic Ramayana, in a manuscript dated about AD 1045 written by the Iranian geographer Al-Biruni. The story tells how Ravana abducts Sita, the wife of Rama, and takes her to Lanka. Rama with an army of apes attacks the labyrinth-castle of Lanka, kills Ravana and frees his wife. After the victory Rama and Sita leave Lanka in Ravana's chariot, significantly making seven circuits around the fortress.

Before investigating the physical evidence, it is worth considering the characteristics of a maze or labyrinth. Strictly, labyrinth implies a single path and ritual aspects, whilst maze tends to be a puzzle, with junctions and choices. In practice these two English words are often used interchangeably, so it is safest to consider them as two variations of the same word. There is less confusion in other languages where the word '*labyrinthe*' covers all kinds.

A spiral is not a maze, nor are complicated buildings, narrow streets, cultivation patterns or intertwining freeways, although the word maze is a widely used metaphor. Yet our ability to recognize maze-like qualities in such a variety of settings reflects its compelling nature.

A maze or labyrinth has various hallmarks. It contains twists and turns, such as definite angles or hairpin bends, so smooth spirals are excluded. It is humanly devised, which eliminates caves and other naturally occuring phenomena. It posseses a deliberate and pleasing design, either as an artefact, or to function as a puzzle, or both. The visitor experiences apparent purpose and progress, however misguided. If a maze is built full size, it can accommodate a considerable number of people, and is easy to use.

Although smooth progress in straight lines or steady curves is repeatedly disrupted by the design, a maze is fundamentally intended for movement. This is as compelling as the onward and relentless pace of time, and as vital as a shark's need to keep moving through water or else die. There are certain optional characteristics. Multicursal (many-pathed) mazes have junctions, whilst unicursal (single-pathed) mazes do not. Many maze designs seem to be

symmetrical, although none have absolute symmetry. If there is a key to solving the maze, then it should be easy to grasp and remember.

A modern maze often has further qualities. It can be a deviously challenging puzzle, pushing the mathematics and topology of mazes to its limits. The design can include carefully chosen materials, to contribute to its setting and enhance the landscape. It may aim to capture visitors' imagination by the use of imagery and symbolism, so that the satisfaction of solving the puzzle is heightened by discovering the hidden meanings.

The earliest physical labyrinth is not known. One candidate might seem to be the giant labyrinthine structure built at Fayum in Egypt by King Amenemhet III around 1800 BC. Herodotus, born around 484 BC, was the first to use the term 'labyrinth' to describe its 'twelve courts, all of them roofed, with gates exactly opposite one another, six looking to the north, and six looking to the south', with winding paths leading from court to chamber, and from chamber into colonnades. Its lower floor, with three thousand chambers and countless pillars, was a sanctuary for the sacred crocodiles and the burial place for kings. However, it was only labyrinthine in the sense of being extensive and confusing, and lacks the tightly coiled paths and deliberate design of a true labyrinth. Little more than its site now remains.

EARLY EXAMPLES OF CLASSICAL SEVEN-RING LABYRINTHS

'Tomba del Labirinto', Luzzanas, Sardinia; rock carving 2500–2000 BC or possibly later
Tell Rifa'at, Syria; ceramic vessel, *c.* 1300 BC
Pylos, Greece; clay tablet *c.* 1200 BC
Padugula, Nilgiri Hills, Tamil Nadu, South India; *c.* 1000 BC
Val Camonica, Capo di Ponte, Italy; rock carvings, 1000–500 BC
Pontevedra, north-west Spain; rock carvings, 900–500 BC
Gordion, Turkey; two graffiti, 650 BC?
Tragliatella, Italy; Oinochoe di Tragliatella, ceramic vessel, shows two horsemen and 'TRUIA' reversed, *c.* 600 BC
Athens, Greece; roofing tile, *c.* 400 BC
Knossos, Crete; coins, 430–67 BC
Itanion, Crete; seal, 350–279 BC
Kom Ombo, Egypt; graffito, *c.* 30 BC
Pompeii, Italy; graffito, prior to AD 67
The Hollywood Stone, Ireland; *c.* AD 550 (earliest dateable labyrinth in the British Isles)
'Rosaring', Lassa, Uppland, Sweden; stone-lined path labyrinth, *c.* AD 815 (earliest dateable labyrinth in Scandinavia)
Casa Grande, Arizona, USA; graffito, AD 1100–1200

This Etruscan terracotta winejar from Tragliatella, Italy, shows a procession including seven soldiers carrying shields and two armed horsemen, apparently emerging from a labyrinth, significantly marked with the word TRUIA. *On the other side of the labyrinth are two couples making love.*

Labyrinths go back in history at least four thousand years. For the first three thousand years they were unicursal labyrinths, consisting of a single convoluted path, without junctions. These labyrinths were not puzzles, but instead were intended for ritual walking, running and processions.

The earliest surviving labyrinths, all of the Classical seven-ring design, are rock carvings and graffiti and patterns on coins, seals and ceramic vessels, rather than being to a scale that could be walked upon. Most forms of full-size labyrinth are too vulnerable to survive thousands of years against the combination of neglect, waves of barbarism, and erosion and overgrowth in all but the driest climates.

The earliest attested dates for a surviving labyrinth design are of a ceramic vessel (*c.* 1300 BC) found at Tell Rifa'at, Syria, and an inscribed clay tablet (*c.* 1200 BC) found at Pylos, Peleponnesos, Greece. There are many surviving labyrinths carved on rock faces in Europe which could be older, but adequate dating methods have yet to be devised. The labyrinth carving found inside the 'Tomba del Labirinto', a Neolithic tomb at Luzzanas, Sardinia, could conceivably date to 2500 BC if it is contemporary with the tomb, but later burials make this uncertain.

A labyrinth symbol carved on part of an ancient dolmen at Padugula, Nilgiri Hills, in southern India may date back to *c.* 1000 BC. There are numerous labyrinths in the Tamil Nadu district, carved on dolmens and Hindu temples, illustrated in early manuscripts, and created in stone, similar to those in Scandinavia; to this day, the labyrinth design is chalked on doorway thresholds to keep out evil spirits.

Egyptian seals of the Eighth Dynasty (c. 2400 BC) showing labyrinthine patterns.

There are at least five labyrinths carved into rockfaces above the town of Capo di Ponte, Val Camonica, in northern Italy. They have been ascribed to the late Bronze Age or early Iron Age, *c.* 1000–500 BC. One example has a long necked bird carved beside it, which might be a crane bird. A number of rock carvings of a similar age, *c.* 900–500 BC, again carved with animals alongside, have been found at Pontevedra in north-west Spain.

Various Cretan coins between 430 and 67 BC bore the Classical seven-ring labyrinth design, both in square and circular forms. As durable metal coinage, they could have travelled far and wide in seaborne trade, thus spreading the labyrinth symbol although there is no evidence of this.

At Pompeii, a seven-ring labyrinth was scratched onto a crimson painted pillar in the House of Lucretius, some time before the city was destroyed by the eruption of Vesuvius in AD 79. It has around it the cryptic words *Labyrinthus, hic habitat Minotaurus*. This square-shaped labyrinth is made entirely of straight lines, which are much easier to scratch than concentric curves. This example demonstrates that the Romans were aware of the Classical seven-ring labyrinth, although their most enduring labyrinths were in mosaic, of a later design form.

The inscribed clay tablet (c. 1200 BC) found at Pylos, Peleponnesos, with Linear B text on one side and a square seven-ring labyrinth on the other.

ABOVE *The Cretan labyrinth graffiti traced onto the pillar in the House of Lucretius, Pompeii. It is around 2000 years old.*

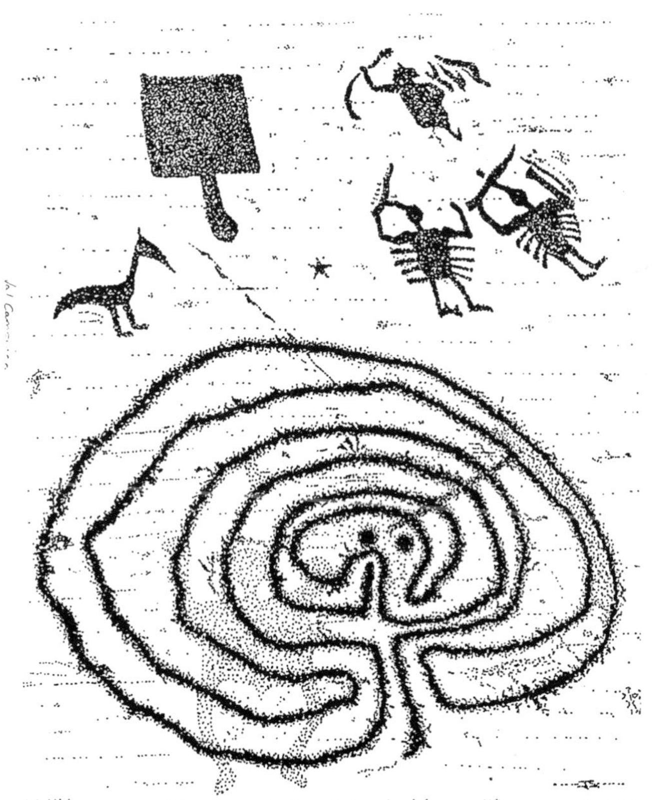

Labyrinth and crane dance, found at Val Camonica. c. 1300–1800 BC.

OPPOSITE *The maze at Trojaburg near Visby, Island of Gotland, Sweden is made of stone-lined paths. Ominously, it lies at the foot of Gallows Hill. This is one of the nearly forty stone labyrinths on the island of Gotland.*

Despite Britain's abundant Neolithic and Bronze Age rock carvings, especially in northern England, Scotland and Ireland, there are very few examples of ancient labyrinthine carvings. Rock carvings found at Newgrange, Co. Meath, at Seskilgreen, Co. Tyrone, and at Ballygowan, Argyll, Scotland all have a labyrinthine character, although none are true Classical seven-ring labyrinths. The earliest dateable labyrinth in the British Isles, *c.* AD 550, is the Hollywood Stone found in the Wicklow Mountains in Ireland. The two Classical seven-ring labyrinth rock carvings in the Rocky Valley near Tintagel, Cornwall, have sharply cut grooves and are cut at a fairly constant angle, suggesting they were made with an iron tool. Two widely differing but plausible dates are the early sixth century when the Christian missionary St Nectan occupied a monastic cell up the valley, and the late seventeenth century when an eccentric millowner, a brilliant but illiterate mathematician, built the now-ruined mill.

THE HOLLYWOOD STONE

The Hollywood Stone, now in the Museum of Antiquities, Dublin.

The Hollywood Stone, *c.* AD 550, is the oldest dateable labyrinth in the British Isles. It was found buried directly beside St Kevin's Road, a pilgrim track leading from Hollywood to the early Celtic monastic settlement at Glendalough. Its significant location was at the narrow point at the start of a tortuous fourteen-mile pathway through the Wicklow Mountains. Its labyrinthine design may have been a waymark, as well as a symbol of both the tortuous physical and spiritual journeys ahead. This is interesting evidence of the labyrinth in Ireland, long before its possible introduction by Saxons or Vikings.

In Scandinavia, there are over five hundred stone-lined path labyrinths, mostly along the shores of the Baltic Sea. Over three hundred are in Sweden, with more than one hundred and fifty in Finland, over sixty in the Soviet Union, over twenty in Norway, and four in Iceland. The entire land mass of Scandinavia has been rising since the last ice age, so labyrinths close to the coast must be medieval or later, as earlier they would have been underwater.

There are over twenty labyrinths which could be pre-medieval, possibly as early as the Bronze Age; these are far inland and high above sea level, and their sites are associated with ancient barrows, cairns and graves. The earliest Scandinavian labyrinth that can be reasonably dated is the 'Rosaring' in Lassa parish in Uppland, Sweden, *c.* AD 815; it has seven rings of stone-lined paths. In the Solovecke Archipelago, there is an interesting group of labyrinths, apparently related to cairns and rock carvings which have been tentatively dated by Soviet archaeologists to *c.* 4000 BC. However, the great majority of

'Troy Town' on St Agnes, Scilly Isles, is thought to have been built by a lighthouse keeper in 1729.

the Scandinavian stone labyrinths are medieval or later, since they are found near sea level on coasts or on offshore islands, often more accessible by boat than by any other means.

England is thought to have once contained over a hundred unicursal turf mazes. There is a correlation between the areas invaded by Nordic settlers during the Dark Ages, and the places where turf labyrinths were created. Place names where turf mazes were created, such as Wing, Asenby and Brandsby, have Nordic origins. The turf maze at Dalby in North Yorkshire and the private turf maze at Somerton in Oxfordshire are the only remaining British examples of the Classical design in turf.

Germany also has a tradition of turf mazes, with a strong emphasis on Whitsun and the month of May. Turf labyrinths of the Classical design can be found at Graitschen and Steigra. Both have traditions of being created by Swedish soldiers during the Thirty Years War (1618–48), and their names indicate a connection with the burial of Swedish officers, but they are both widely thought to be older. The turf labyrinth at Graitschen was named 'Schwedenhieb' (Swede's cut) or 'Schwedenhugel' (Swede's hill), and its design appears within the official seal of the village. The Steigra maze was known as 'Schwedengang' (Swede's path) or 'Schwedenring' (Swede's ring), and during the nineteenth century, its maintenance was carried out each year on the third day of Whitsun by young people who had been confirmed into the Christian faith.

A significant variation to the Classical labyrinth design is the addition of a second entrance (or exit), so that a procession can enter by one entrance, reach the centre, and then emerge by a short exit without turning round. The design is still essentially unicursal.

Design of the maze at Ripon Common which followed the medieval Christian pattern. It is now destroyed.

ABOVE *The turf maze at Steigra, whose name 'Schwedenring' dates back to the Thirty Years War, follows the Classical labyrinth design.*

ABOVE LEFT *The private turf maze at Troy Farm, Somerton, Oxfordshire.*

LEFT *The Dalby turf maze lies beside the road in the Yorkshire Wolds, between the villages of Dalby and Brandsby. Its seven-ring Classical design suggests great antiquity. This eastern part of England was invaded by Norsemen in the dark ages; Viking York is only a few miles away, and Dalby is an ancient place name.*

This processional type of maze is found in both Scandinavia and northern Europe. At the 'Windelbahn' turf maze at Stolp in Pomerania, the journeymen of the shoemaker's guild held a Whitsun festival every third year, led by an elected 'Maigraf' (May king), which included a long procession through the labyrinth to the goal and out by its short exit. The 'Rad' (Wheel) turf labyrinth in the Eilenreide forest near Hanover is also of the processional type. It was already well established by 1642, when it is recorded that Duke Christian Ludwig entertained his brother-in-law Duke Friedrich of Holstein and his newly-married wife in the forest for two days, living in tents, shooting, and playing games in the labyrinth.

Although not in the Classical design, the labyrinth motif was used in mosaic pavements throughout the Roman Empire. They are the oldest surviving group of full-size labyrinths. As well as being durable, they were often protected from further erosion by the collapse of the very buildings they once adorned, and thus many examples have survived.

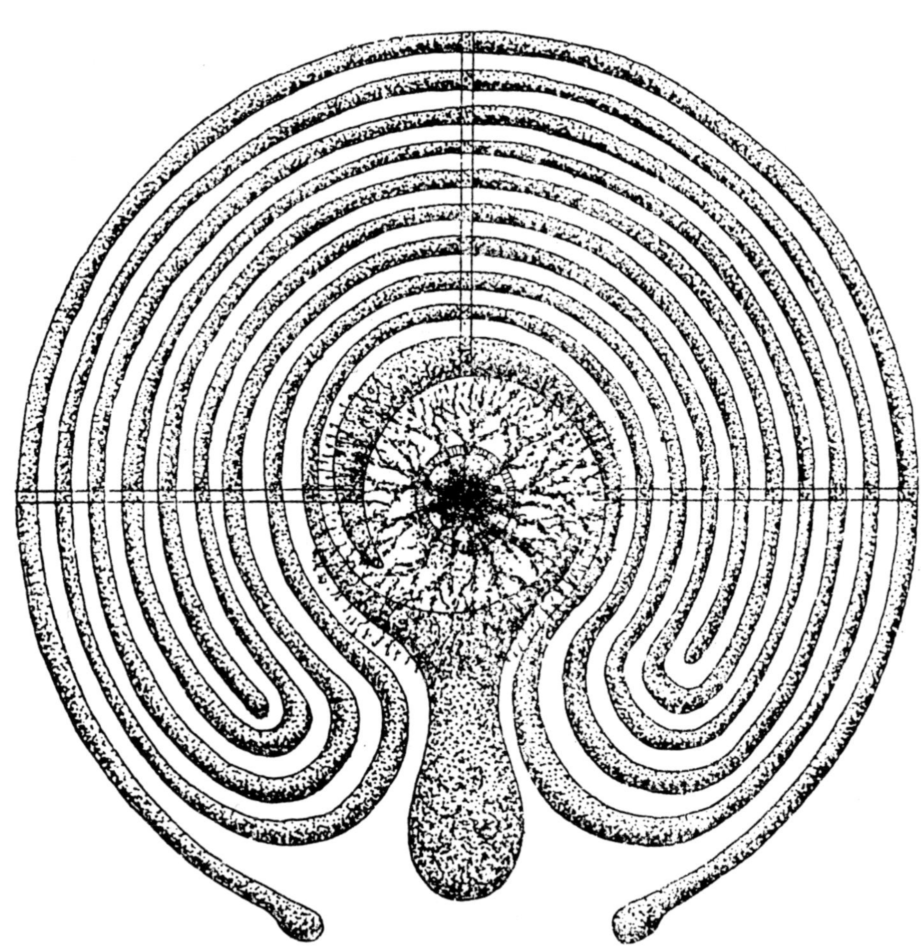

Over 105 feet in diameter, the 'Rad' in the Eilenreide forest is one of the most impressive turf labyrinths in Europe.

The central rondel of a mosaic pavement maze in the Museo de Navarra, Pamplona, showing Theseus fighting the Minotaur.

The medium of mosaic offers great scope to maze design. In Roman times, mosaic mazes consisted of a rectangular grid of tesserae for most of their area, though only taking full advantage of the pictorial scope of mosaic for a central illustration. Normally square and the size of a room, the most popular subject was Theseus slaying the Minotaur, but some Roman labyrinths simply portrayed the Minotaur, or other half-human creatures such as centaurs. The paths of Roman labyrinths methodically filled one quarter at a time, before repeating the pattern in the next quarter and so on.

Fine mosaic labyrinths have been found throughout the Roman Empire. There is a magnificent labyrinth pavement found at a Roman villa near Salzburg (now in Vienna) with four illustrations, showing Theseus slaying the Minotaur, Ariadne and Theseus joining hands over an altar, Theseus putting Ariadne ashore, and finally the deserted Ariadne alone on the Island of Naxos. There is also a splendid circular mosaic at Fribourg in Switzerland, with eight axes, four elegant towers, eight attentive birds and Theseus and the Minotaur at the centre. The circular mosaic labyrinth at Kato Paphos in Cyprus is exquisite, with minute detail to the paths and an elaborate central mosaic with five carefully portrayed figures.

In Britain, square Roman mosaic labyrinths have been found at Cirencester, Caerleon and Harpham. At Oldcotes in Nottinghamshire, there is a buried labyrinth showing Theseus and the Minotaur at its centre, with a labyrinth

The Roman mosaic found near Salzburg, Austria, now in the Kunsthistorisches Museum, Vienna. The cameos illustrate the story of Theseus and the Minotaur.

ABOVE *The mosaic maze found at Calvatone, near Piadena, Italy.*

ABOVE LEFT *The Roman mosaic maze with bastions discovered in 1957 in the Via Cadolini, Cremona.*

design said to be almost identical to the one at Caerleon. Also in Cirencester is a second labyrinthine example, this time a labyrinth border around a central mosaic. There is also a very crudely designed mosaic labyrinth at Fullerton.

The earliest Christian maze is probably that in the fourth-century basilica of Reparatus, Orleansville in Algeria. The design of this pavement maze is in the methodical Roman style, progressing one quarter at a time. The words SANCTA ECLESIA at the centre emphasize its Christian purpose.

The great breakthrough, however, was in the development of the medieval Christian labyrinth design. This had eleven rings instead of seven, a characteristic cruciform design, and most significantly, the paths ranged freely through the quadrants, rather than methodically proceeding quarter by quarter in the Roman way. A manuscript in the Vatican dated AD 860–2 contains a prototype of this innovatory medieval Christian design, and the tenth-century Montpellier manuscript portrays the design more formally. It was executed in two main forms, circular and octagonal.

The earliest surviving example built full size dates back to 1235, within the pavement of the nave of Chartres Cathedral; it is circular, and was known as '*Chemin de Jerusalem*'. There is a smaller circular pavement labyrinth at

ROMAN MOSAIC LABYRINTHS

Algeria

Annaba, Algeria; rectangular; head of Minotaur at centre, 3 × 3 ft

Caesarea, Cherchel, Algeria; square, 6 × 6 ft; *c.* 200 AD; only partial remains

Dellys, Algeria; black and white mosaic labyrinth; square, 13 × 13 ft; *c.* 200 AD; severely damaged

Orleansville, Algeria; in Church of Reparatus; square labyrinth, with SANCTA ECLESIA repeatedly at centre; 8 × 8 ft; probably fourth century AD

Tametfoust/Bordi el-Bahri (formerly Rusguniae), Algeria; black and white mosaic labyrinth; octagonal, 11 × 11 ft; fourth century AD; still *in situ*.

Tigzirt-sur-Mer (formerly Iomnium), Algeria; black and white square mosaic labyrinth; *c.* 450 AD

Austria

Salzburg (formerly Juvavum), Austria; found in Roman villa at Loig; now in Kunsthistorisches Museum, Vienna; magnificent polychrome square mosaic labyrinth with four illustrated panels; originally 21 × 18 ft; *c.* 275–300 AD

Britain

Caerleon-on-Usk Legionary Museum, Gwent, Wales; fine example, square; 8 × 8 ft; second/third century AD

Cirencester, Gloucestershire; labyrinth border, square; 15 × 15 ft; second century AD

Cirencester, Gloucestershire; fine example, square; 6 × 6 ft; early fourth century AD

Fullerton, Hampshire; very crude design, square; 12 × 12 ft; fourth century AD

Harpham, East Yorkshire; fine example, square, now in Hull City Hall; 12 × 12 ft; fourth century AD

Oldcotes, Nottinghamshire; polychrome mosaic labyrinth; square, 9 × 9 ft; third century AD; mosaic now reburied

Cyprus

Kato Paphos, Cyprus; small circular mosaic labyrinth, 1′ 6″ × 1′ 6″; second century AD

Kato Paphos, Cyprus; rolling rope mosaic labyrinth path, and magnificent portrayal of Minotaur legend at centre; circular, 20 × 20 ft; *c.* 350 AD

France

Aix-en-Provence, France; labyrinth with combat of Theseus and Minotaur at centre; 18 × 12 ft; found 1790

Chusclan, Gard, France; labyrinth with seven towers; 10 × 10 ft; second century

Gard, France; in Saint-Come-et-Maruejols; crude square labyrinth design, 3 ft 6 in × 5 ft 3 ins

Lyon, France; in Musée de la Civilisation Gallo-Romaine; polychrome mosaic with four corner towers and eight birds; circular, 34 × 20 ft; *c.* 200–250 AD

Lyons, France; in Sainte-Colombe

Nîmes, France; mosaic labyrinth found in Le Mas Foulc, now in Archaeological Museum; unusual asymmetric design; square, 1 ft 6 ins × 1 ft 6 ins; *c.* 100 AD

Pont-Chevron, nr Ouzouer-sur-Trezee, Loiret, France; black and white square mosaic labyrinth, 3 × 3 ft; second century AD; still *in situ*

Verdes, Blois, Loir-et-Cher, France; in Roman baths; circular with eight bold and detailed towers; 33 × 30 ft; *c.* 200–250 AD

Greece

Sparta, Greece; labyrinthine meanders in polychrome mosaic, still *in situ*; square, 13 × 13 ft; *c.* 250 AD

Italy

Brindisi; 17 ft × 10 ft 6 ins; sixteen perimeter towers; *c.* 200–250 AD

Piadena, nr Cremona (formerly Betriacum), Italy; found at Calvatone; black and white mosaic labyrinth with eight small towers and battlements; square, 4 × 4 ft; *c.* 25–50 AD

Cremona, Italy; found in villa in Via Cadolini; black and white mosaic labyrinth with six bold towers and battlements; square, 5 × 4 ft; first century AD

Giannutri, Italy; black and white mosaic labyrinth; square, 13 × 15 ft; second century AD; incomplete

Nora, Sardinia; polychrome mosaic labyrinth, *c.* 200 AD; only fragments remain; still *in situ*

Ostia, Rome, Italy; black and white mosaic labyrinth; square, 15 × 15 ft; *c.* 150 AD

Pompeii, Italy; found in House of the Labyrinth; black and white mosaic labyrinth; square, 7 × 7 ft;

c. 80–60 BC; still *in situ*

Pompeii, Italy; found in Villa of Diomede; magnificent square labyrinth with sixteen perimeter towers; *c.* 80–60 BC

Pompeii, Italy; black and white mosaic labyrinth; square, 7 × 7 ft; *c.* 60–40 BC; still *in situ*

Pompeii, Italy; in a private house; square; *c.* 50 BC

Rome, Italy; found in a private house in Piazza San Giovanni in Laterano; polychrome mosaic labyrinth portraying sixteen towers and perimeter wall; square, about 13 ft × 13 ft; *c.* 100–80 BC

Rome, Italy; near Piramide di Cestio; labyrinthine meanders in black and white mosaic; originally square, only 8 × 4 ft remains; first century AD

Rome, Italy; Sant'Agata in Petra Aurea; black and white mosaic labyrinth, 23 × 16 ft; *c.* 130 AD

Selinunte (formerly Soluntum), Sicily; circular labyrinth; *c.* 125–100 BC; only a fragment remains

Syracuse, Sicily; in a private house in Taormina; black and white mosaic labyrinth; square, 21 × 20 ft; *c.* 150 AD; incomplete remains

Libya

Cirene, Libya; square polychrome labyrinth, 25 × 17 ft; *c.* 200 AD

Sabrata, Libya; black and white mosaic labyrinth, with woven border; circular, 10 × 10 ft; first century AD

Portugal

Coimbra Museum, Portugal; black and white mosaic square labyrinth, decorated with eight towers and central bust of Minotaur; 11 × 10 ft; second century AD

Coimbra, Portugal; polychrome mosaic square labyrinth central bust of Minotaur; 11 × 10 ft; second century AD

Spain

Altafulla, Tarragona, Spain; *c.* 230 AD

Cordova, Spain; polychrome mosaic; 14 × 13 ft; *c.* 150–200 AD

Pamplona, Spain; in Museo de Navarra; black and white mosaic labyrinth, with Theseus and Minotaur at centre; circular; *c.* 150 AD; central fragment remains

Italica, near Seville, Spain; Roman villa 'Casa del Labyrinto'; rolling rope motif in polychrome mosaic; sixteen towers, with Theseus and Minotaur at centre; 21 × 12 ft; *c.* 150 AD

Switzerland

Avrenches Museum, Avrenches, Switzerland; circular, decorated with tower motif; 2 × 2 ft; *c.* 250 AD

Baugy, near Vevey, Switzerland; circular

Cormerod, Canton of Friburg, Switzerland; displayed in University of Friburg; circular eight-axis mosaic labyrinth with bird decoration; originally 20 × 14 ft; *c.* 200–225 AD

Orbe, Canton of Vaud, Switzerland; still *in situ*, mosaic labyrinth surrounded by four corner towers and four gateways; square, 12 × 12 ft; *c.* 200 AD

Tunisia

El-Djem (formerly Thysdrus), Tunisia; black and white mosaic labyrinth with four fine towers and perimeter battlements; circular, 8 × 8 ft; *c.* 175–225 AD; incomplete remains

Henchir el-Faouar (formerly Belalis Major), Tunisia; square mosaic labyrinth with four towers, 16 × 16 ft; fourth century AD

Mactar (formerly Mactaris), Tunisia; huge semicircular stone labyrinth, 54 × 25 ft; 199 AD

Susa (formerly Hadrumetum), Tunisia; black and white square mosaic labyrinth, with text *Hic inclusus vitam perdit* and ship entering; total pavement 18 × 11 ft; *c.* 200–250 AD; now destroyed

Tunis, Tunisia; fine polychrome mosaic labyrinth; square, 16 × 16 ft; second century AD; section remains

Tunis, Tunisia; in Roman villa at Henchir Kasbat (formerly Thuburbo Maius); black and white mosaic labyrinth; square, 12 × 10 ft; *c.* 300 AD

Yugoslavia

Gamzigrad, Yugoslavia; hexagonal, with six corner towers and perimeter wall; 9 × 9 ft; *c.* 300 AD

Pula (Pola), Yugoslavia; in Roman villa; black and white labyrinth surrounded by sixteen towers; square, 14 × 14 ft; *c.* 200 AD; still *in situ*

Sarajevo Museum, Yugoslavia; from Roman baths of Stolac; polychrome labyrinth with four towers and four doorways; square, 14 × 14 ft; *c.* 300 AD

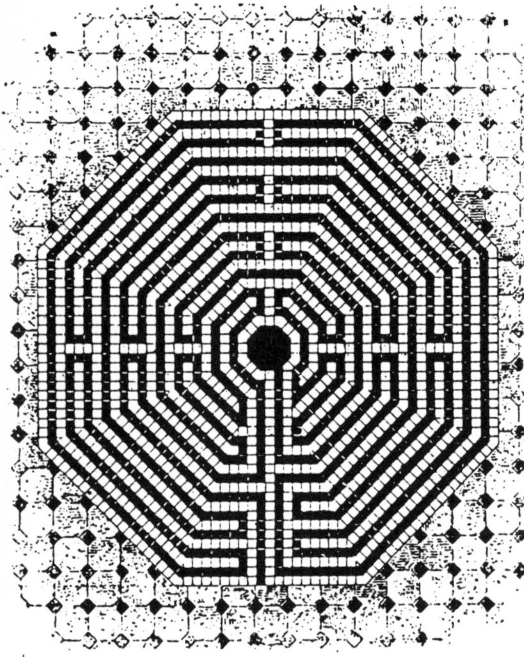

ABOVE *The design of the octagonal pavement maze at St Quentin.*

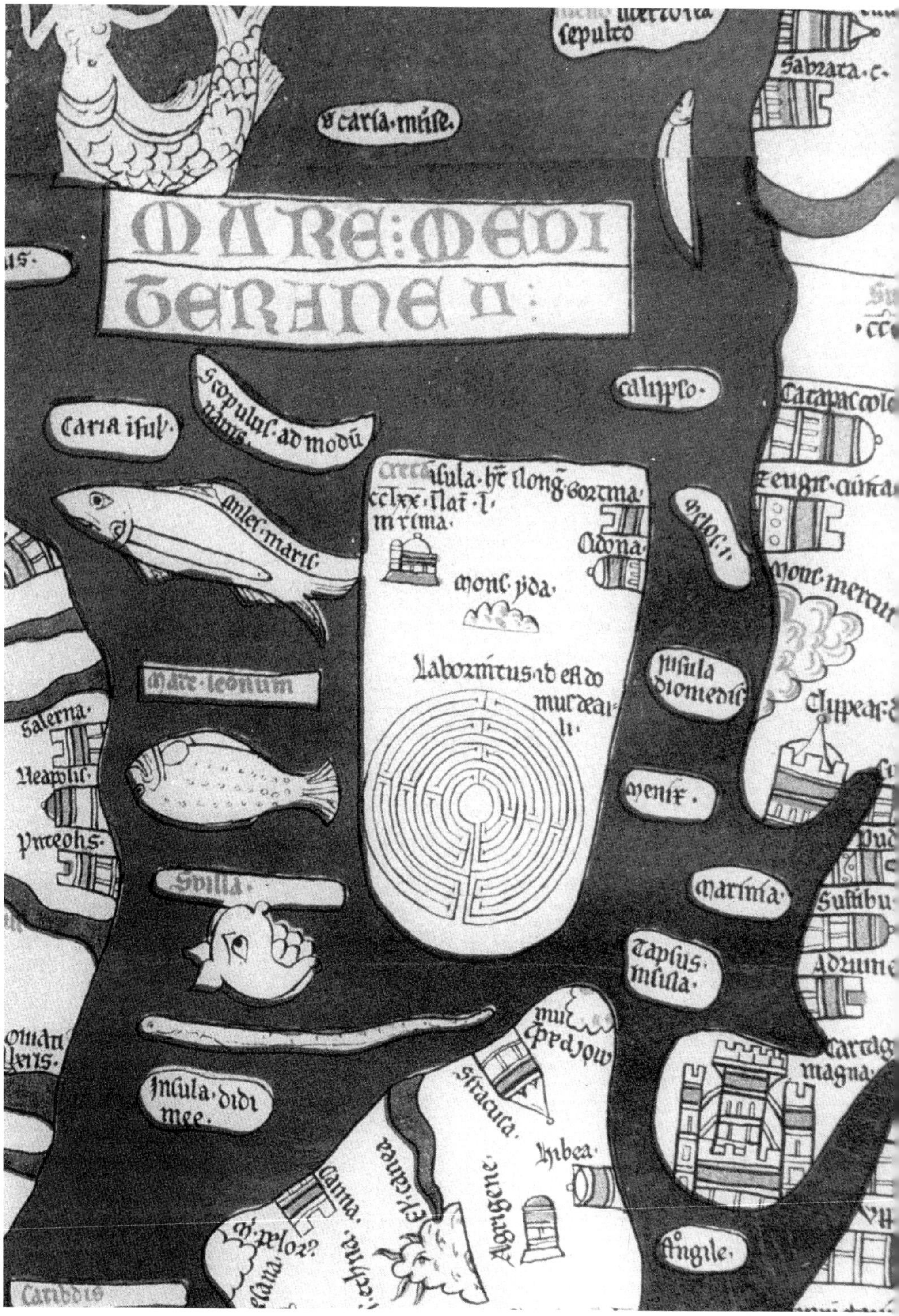

The maze on the thirteenth-century Mappa Mundi follows the medieval Christian design. It is used to signify Crete.

The pavement maze in Amiens Cathedral is strikingly laid in shades of marble.

Bayeux, and formerly there was one at Sens. Beautiful octagonal examples are found in the cathedrals of Amiens and St Quentin; octagonal labyrinths with the addition of four corner bastions were created at Rheims Cathedral and Genainville, although only the latter has survived.

These stone pavement mazes were originally confined to the gothic cathedrals of northern France. This new labyrinth design was introduced together with rose windows and elegant flying buttresses, using the latest advances in glass, accurate stonework and precise mathematical calculation. These Christian labyrinths represented the Path of Life and reflected the recent journeys of the Crusades, with the centre symbolizing the reaching of both Jerusalem and Salvation. They tended to be located towards the west end of the nave, and were therefore accessible for lay people to walk or kneel their way along the path.

The medieval Christian design is also found carved vertically; the inscribed pillar in Lucca cathedral is rather ill-formed, and may have been formalized from an initial graffito, whilst the fifteenth-century wall labyrinth at St Lawrence Church, Rathmore, Co. Meath is more deliberate since the incised barriers project the path outwards.

In England, the medieval Christian design was not applied within gothic church buildings. However, it did appear widely in the form of turf mazes. A suggested explanation is that turf labyrinths were already widespread, but laid out in the Classical design, with names such as Shepherd's Race and Robin Hood's Race (which imply vigorous running rather than a predominantly spiritual purpose). There were also names such as Julian's Bower, Maiden's Bower and Walls of Troy, identical to labyrinth names found in Scandinavia. For Christianity to prevail at these places of pre-Christian activity, turf mazes may have been recut to the medieval Christian design, thus allowing the same maze sites to be used with the blessing of the Church. For example the village of Wing derives its place-name from the norse *Vengi*, which pre-dates the medieval Christian design of its turf maze by several centuries.

In Germany, turf labyrinths traditionally seem to have been recut and used by young people each spring, although these springtime customs do not seem directly related to Christianity. Only later did the Christian calendar establish its connection with these mazes, so that they were recut at Whitsuntide.

The turf mazes at Alkborough and Hilton are both deeply sunk below the level of the surrounding ground – at Alkborough by a couple of feet. The repeated scouring out of the channels can gradually cause the level of a maze to sink, like an ancient track, so perhaps these sunken turf mazes are of great antiquity. In Britain, only eight ancient turf mazes have survived, from over one hundred known sites of former turf mazes. Similarly in Germany, only three survive from over a dozen known sites.

RIGHT *Labyrinth incised upon one of the porch piers of Lucca Cathedral.*

FAR RIGHT *Fifteenth-century wall labyrinth at St Lawrence Church, Rathmore, Co. Meath in Ireland.*

MEDIEVAL CHRISTIAN LABYRINTHS, 12th–16th CENTURIES

Surviving

Amiens Cathedral, Somme, France; medieval Christian stone pavement labyrinth; octagonal, 40 × 40 ft: built 1288, destroyed 1825–28, restored 1894

Bayeux Cathedral, France; labyrinth of red, black and encaustic tiles, laid in the floor of the chapter house; circular, 12 × 12 ft; thirteenth century

Bristol, Avon, England; in St Mary Redcliffe church; medieval Christian labyrinth design; circular carved wooden boss, 8 × 8 ins; fifteenth century

Chartres Cathedral, France; blue and white stone pavement labyrinth, medieval Christian design, with six apses at centre; circular, 41 × 40 ft; built 1235

Genainville church, Val-d'Oise, France; vertical stone carving; octagonal medieval Christian design with bastions, 2 ft 6 in × 2 ft; fourteenth century

Ghent Town Hall, Belgium; white and blue stone, to similar labyrinth design as St Omer; rectangular, 46 × 39 ft; designed by Walter van Werveke, 1528

Lucca Cathedral, Italy; vertical carving on stone pillar; medieval Christian labyrinth design; circular, 1 ft 6 in × 1 ft 6 in; twelfth century

Mappa Mundi, Hereford Cathedral, Herefordshire, England; depiction of labyrinth on island of Crete, drawn by Richard de Bello; 5 × 4 ft; *c.* 1280 AD

Mirepoix Cathedral, Mirepoix, France; medieval Christian labyrinth design on nine floor tiles, with central Minotaur; circular, 2 × 2 ft; built *c.* 1497–1537

Orleans, France; church of S. Euverte; black and white tiles, similar labyrinth design to St Omer; square, 30 × 30 ft; thirteenth century

Pavia, Italy; semi-circular labyrinth on wall of San Michele Maggiore church; twelfth century; fragment remains

Ravenna, Italy; in church of San Vitale; coloured marble pavement labyrinth; circular, 11 × 11 ft; laid 1584

Rathmore, Co. Meath, Eire; in St Lawrence's Church; medieval Christian labyrinth design, carved in stone; circular, 14 × 14 ins; mid-fifteenth century

Rome, Italy; church of Sta Maria-di-Trastavera; coloured marble labyrinth, incorrectly restored; circular, 11 × 11 ft; late twelfth century

St Quentin parish church, France; blue/black and white stone medieval Christian labyrinth; octagonal, 35 × 35 ft; built 1495

Toulouse, France; Chappelle de la Prevote; circular labyrinth on nine floor tiles; 2 × 2 ft; built 1439–51

Destroyed

Arras Cathedral, France; medieval Christian pavement labyrinth, of blue and yellow squares; octagonal, 35 × 35 ft; built 1160, destroyed 1793, following the French Revolution

Auxerre, France; in cathedral of Saint-Etienne; circular; built 1334 or 1335, destroyed 1690

Caen, Normandy, France; formerly on floor of guard chamber in Abbey of St Stephen; intricate labyrinth on clay-baked tiles; circular, approx. 10 × 10 ft; pavement destroyed in 1802

Chalons-sur-Marne, France; series of 5 × 5 ins tiles decorated with Classical design labyrinths in Toussaints Abbey; abbey destroyed in 1544

Chambery Cathedral, Chambery, France; elliptical, built *c.* 1625; mentioned in Bulteau's *Monograph.*

Cologne, West Germany; in St Severin Church, medieval Christian pavement labyrinth, built *c.* 1200

Finisterre, France; at Abbaye de Pont l'Abbé; pavement tiles with medieval Christian labyrinth designs; fifteenth or sixteenth century.

Piacenza, Italy; church of S. Savino; circular, with Zodiac signs in juxtaposition; twelfth century

Poitiers, France; 11-ring medieval Christian pavement labyrinth, circular (not oval as frequently cited in error); now only 3 × 3 ft; graffito on wall remains; built in thirteenth century

Rheims Cathedral, France; medieval Christian design; octagonal with four bastions, 33 × 33 ft; built 1211–40; destroyed 1779

Rome, Italy; church of Sta Maria-in-Aquiro; labyrinth of bands of porphyry and yellow and green marble; circular, 5 × 5 ft; laid *c.* 1189, destroyed late nineteenth century

St Omer, France; in Abbey of St Bertin; square, 36 × 36 ft; fourteenth century, destroyed in eighteenth century

Sens Cathedral, France; stone pavement, with incised paths filled with lead; circular, 33 × 33 ft; built twelfth century, destroyed 1768

The village place name of Wing is of ancient origin, going back to the Norse word 'Vengi'. Coming from Scandinavia and its tradition of stone labyrinths, Nordic settlers may have laid out labyrinths in their settlements to remind them of their origins. Lacking stones, they used turf. In the Dark Ages, the Classical design was the only labyrinth design known to them.

BELOW *The design of the maze near St Ann's Well, Sneinton, Nottinghamshire, now destroyed, and known as Robin Hood's Race.*

The turf maze at Hilton.

LEFT OPPOSITE *The word Mizmaze applies to two surviving turf mazes in southern England, at Breamore and at St Catherine's Hill, Winchester. The Breamore mizmaze is thought to have been cut by monks from the nearby monastery, who according to local tradition used it as a place of penance.*

RIGHT *The turf maze of medieval Christian origin at Saffron Walden in Essex.*

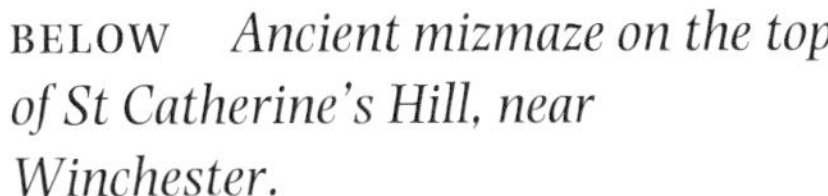

BELOW *Ancient mizmaze on the top of St Catherine's Hill, near Winchester.*

The church has continued to use the labyrinth up to the present day. In the nineteenth century, mazes were created in Ely Cathedral and Bourn Church; the maze in the porch of Guingamp Church, Brittany is probably also of this date. Mr J. Goulton-Constable's interest in the Alkborough turf maze resulted in the installation of its Christian design in a stone pavement in the church porch, in Victorian stained glass within the east end window, and on his own tombstone.

In the late twentieth century, mazes have been created at Batheaston, Avon, and at St Regnus Church, Burt, Co. Donegal. Dr Arnold Wolff created an octagonal labyrinth in Cologne Cathedral in 1977. In South Africa, the Ely design was copied in Pietermaritzburg Cathedral. In her garden at York Gate, Adel, near Leeds, Mrs Sybil Spencer has built a circular medieval Christian maze with granite setts and gravel, with a compass at its centre.

LEFT OPPOSITE *The modern pavement maze in the church at Guingamp, Britanny.*

Maze in the stained glass window of Alkborough Church, Humberside. The design is repeated on a tombstone.

OPPOSITE LEFT *St Regnus church, Burt, Co. Donegal, abounds in symbolism including labyrinthine designs on its doorhandles. This unusual interpretation of the classic labyrinth highlights the cruciform nature of the central intersection.*

LATER CHRISTIAN MAZES

Church mazes, 19th–20th centuries

Alkborough church, South Humberside; copies of village's turf maze design in porch pavement (6 × 6 ft, 1887) and stained glass East window (4 ins wide)

Batheaston church, Avon; copy of pavement maze formerly in Abbey of St Omer; 16 × 16 ft; built by Rev. Paul Lucas, 1985

Bourn church, Cambridgeshire; in red and white tiles, 15 × 12 ft, 1875; rectangular copy Hampton Court maze design

Burt, Co. Donegal, Eire; in St Regnus church; labyrinthine panels and door handles, *c.* 1967

Cologne Cathedral, West Germany; black and white marble labyrinth, octagonal, 4 × 4 ft; designed by Dr Arnold Wolff, 1977

Compton, Surrey, England; in Watts Memorial Chapel; four corbels of labyrinth-bearing angels, and a gilded labyrinth carved on altar; *c.* 1896

Ely Cathedral, Cambridgeshire; square pavement, 20 × 20 ft, designed by Sir Gilbert Scott, 1870

Guingamp church, Brittany, France; circular pavement labyrinth, with 'Ave Maria' and Fleur de Lys at centre; 18 × 18 ft; nineteenth century

Hadstock churchyard, Essex, England; 18 inch wide bronze replica of Arkville labyrinth on tombstone of Michael Ayrton, who died in 1975

Itchen Stoke, Hampshire, England; in St Mary's church; pavement maze beneath altar, in russet and green tiles; circular, 15 ft; *c.* 1866

Mailly-Maillet, France; in church of S. Peter; black and white stone rectangular labyrinth, similar in design to St Omer; built in 1927

Pietermaritzburg Cathedral, South Africa; copy of Ely design, 1980

Selestat, Strasbourg, France; in Ste Foy church; red and black medieval Christian pavement labyrinth; octagonal, 23 × 23 ft; built *c.* 1889

Treves Cathedral, Rhenanie-Palatinate, West Germany; blue stone eight-ring labyrinth with rose at centre, circular, 2 × 2 ft

Wyck Rissington church, Gloucestershire, England; memorial wall mosaic, 3 × 2 ft, based on design of former hedge maze in rectory garden; dedicated 1988

Other modern Christian mazes

Archbishop's Maze, Greys Court, Oxfordshire; brick path in grass maze, 85 ft diameter, 1981; based on words of Dr Robert Runcie's enthronement sermon

Arkville Christian Maze, Dry Brook, New York State, USA; octagonal medieval Christian pavement labyrinth in cobbles and brick; built by Michael Ayrton in 1969

Bristol Water Maze, Avon; based on design of fifteenth-century roof boss in St Mary Redcliffe church; built 1984

York Gate, Adel, Leeds, South Yorkshire; granite setts laid in gravel, to medieval Christian design, with central compass

OPPOSITE ABOVE *The mosaic maze created in memory of Canon Harry Cheales, to the same design as the original hedge maze at Wyck Rissington. This mosaic maze within the wall of the north aisle is at a height so that children can trace it with a finger. It was dedicated by the Very Rev. Eric Evans, Dean of St Paul's Cathedral, London in 1988.*

OPPOSITE BELOW *The maze at Hampton Court has been a source of great pleasure and entertainment since it was built in the 1690s, possibly inspired by the Dutch influence brought to England by William and Mary.*

THE MAZE OF THE MYSTERIES OF THE GOSPELS

> The Maze of the Mysteries of the Gospels was originally a hedge maze, created in 1950 by Canon Harry Cheales in the garden of Wyck Rissington rectory in the Cotswolds. Each year on 10 August, the festival of St Lawrence, Canon Cheales led a procession through the maze past carved signs of the fifteen mysteries of the gospels in the correct order. The path led through a signposted tunnel of death ('Life after death – if you don't believe in it, you must turn back here'), into a garden of paradise, through a gate of judgement ('No turning back') to a giant Sequoia tree representing salvation and eternal life. Canon Cheales used the maze as part of his Christian ministry; he was often about the garden, available to talk with visitors who perhaps had discovered something about themselves when solving the maze. Over the years, many hundreds of visitors found themselves challenged by their experiences in this rectory garden maze, and helped by this holy man with all the time in the world.

The Archbishop's Maze at Greys Court, whilst not inside a church, reflects Dr Robert Runcie's dream of a maze, which he described in his sermon when enthroned as Archbishop of Canterbury. In the following year, Dr Runcie came to Greys Court to dedicate the maze, and he composed two special prayers in dedication. The maze, reached by a footbridge over a ha-ha, is a successful addition to a delightful scheme of gardens.

As Europe emerged from the Middle Ages into the Renaissance in the fifteenth century, formal gardens began to be established. Land was enclosed for protection against the foraging of wild animals, and to provide shelter for better cultivation. Puzzle hedge mazes became an amusement of kings and princes, and to start with were only found at the wealthiest palaces. In France, the Roi René, Duc d'Anjou, had a 'daedalus' at the Château de Bauge in 1477. Androuet du Cerceau created a cypress maze in the Tuileries gardens in Paris, and two hedge mazes about 1520 at the Château de Gaillon near Rouen. In the seventeenth century, the royal architects André Mollet and Blondel created labyrinths at Chantilly and Choisy-le-Roi, whilst France's most remarkable hedge labyrinth was created in 1675 for Louis XIV at Versailles. In Holland, the earliest known Dutch maze was at the royal palace of Het Loo, which later inspired the creation of the maze at Hampton Court. In Amsterdam, a hedge maze called 'Dollhuys' was built in 1562 on the Kleevebiers-Burgwal, followed by the 'Oude Doolhof' in 1620, and the 'Nieuwe Doolhof' soon afterwards. In England, a hedge maze at Nonsuch Palace was well established when visited and described in 1599 and one at Theobalds was destroyed in 1643 during the English Civil War. George

Maze in a garden in Rome, 1852.

BELOW *Drawing showing the maze at De Oude Doolhof, Holland, in 1625.*

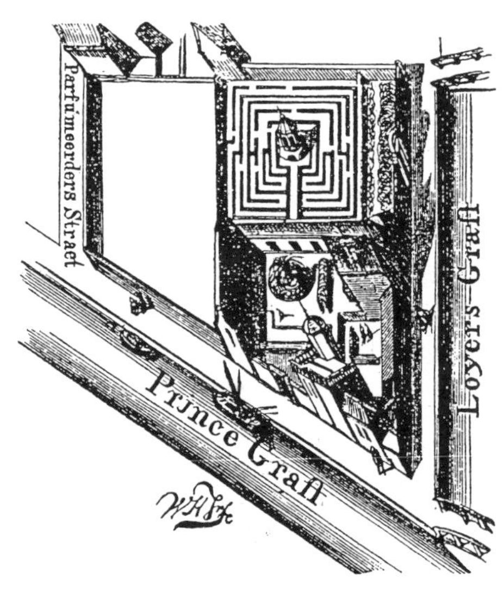

London and Henry Wise planted the hedge maze at Hampton Court Palace between 1689 and 1696, while in Spain, the hedge maze at Seville was originally planted in 1540 for Charles v. Several of the great Italian villas had puzzle hedge mazes, of which the most notable was built in 1720 at the Villa Pisani at Stra.

The English craze for the Italianate gardening style during the 1830s and 1840s led to the creation of a number of mazes, several designed by William Nesfield. During the second half of the nineteenth century, many new puzzle hedge mazes were built in parks and other places, for general public amusement, as well as in the private grounds of the wealthy. The design of the Hampton Court Maze was copied over a dozen times throughout the English-speaking world. In the twentieth century, many mazes were irretrievably lost after five years of enforced neglect during each of the two world wars, and the other economic priorities which followed on each occasion.

LEFT *The hedge maze at Stra was established in 1720 in the garden of the Villa Pisani, twenty-five kilometres south of Venice. Its central tower has two floors and twin spiral staircases, surmounted by a statue of Minerva.*

BELOW *Painting by Tintoretto showing a maze. This painting hangs within Hampton Court Palace.*

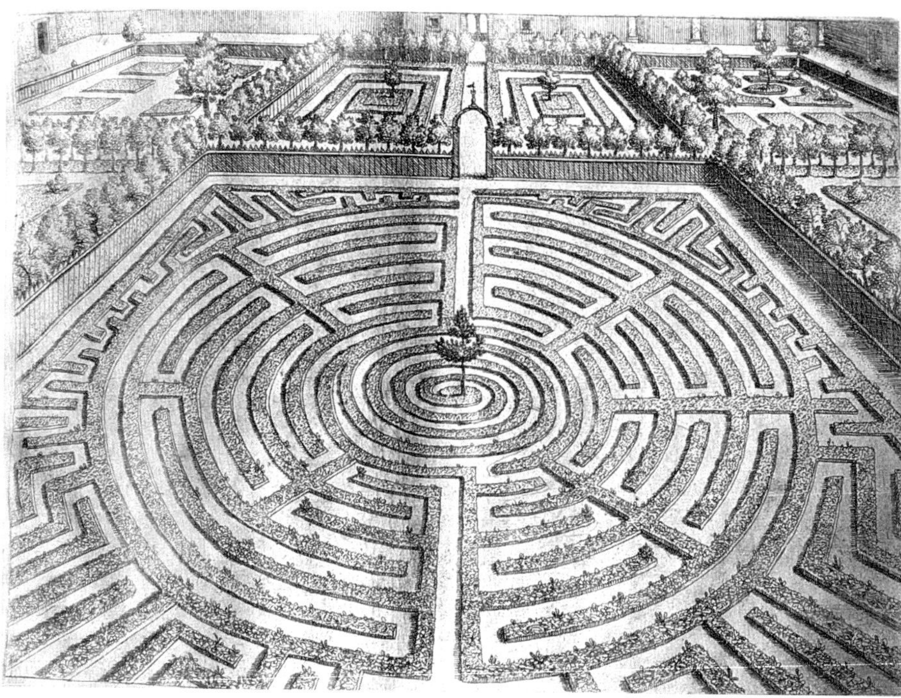

Two drawings showing maze designs from Hortorum vivid ariorumque Formae *by Jan Vredeman de Vries published in Antwerp in 1583.*

Maze at the Emperor's Summer Palace, Yuan Ming Yuan, China. There is no evidence of an independent tradition of mazes in either China or Japan, before the arrival of European influence.

BELOW *Engraving showing the four mazes in the Tivoli Gardens as they were laid out in 1573.*

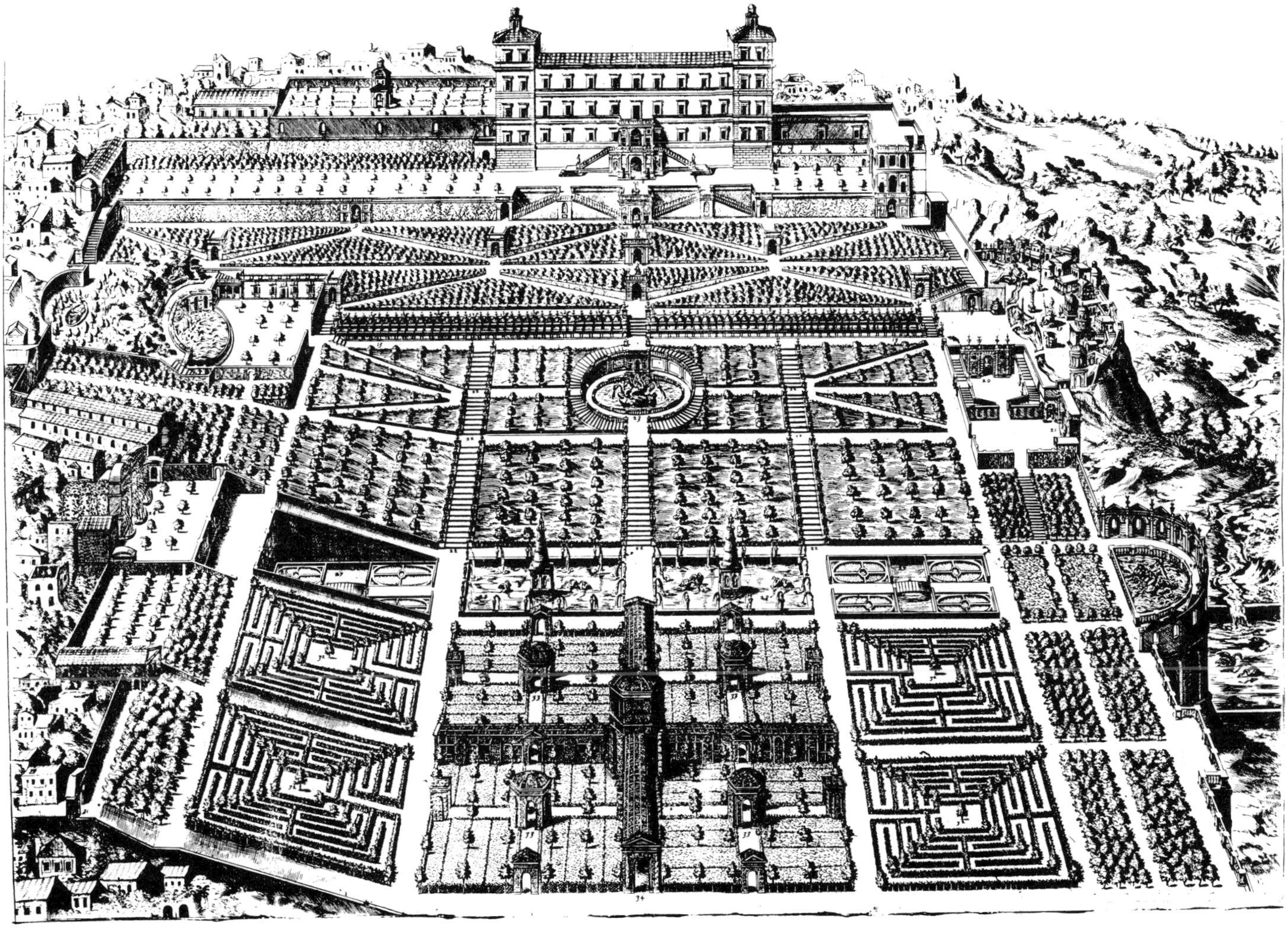

The bronze statue of Icarus, placed within one of two goals at the Arkville Maze, New York State, designed by Michael Ayrton.

Since the 1970s, there has been a revolution in innovative puzzle mazes. Greg Bright's puzzle maze at Longleat had curving paths, wooden bridges, a complete lack of symmetry, and, above all, immense size. Stuart Landsborough's wooden mazes triggered off a maze craze in Japan, resulting in the construction of over two hundred three-dimensional wooden mazes during the 1980s. Our own puzzle innovations have encompassed traditional, interactive and colour mazes, within a diverse range of landscape settings.

The source of innovation in such an esoteric art is sometimes difficult to pin down precisely; some design ideas are conceived long before their practical application is devised. Mazes are essentially a practical art – the acid test is that visitors going through them appreciate the total experience. In the quest for labyrinthine innovation, failures have abounded – technical problems, too little puzzlement, too long a puzzle, too complicated a puzzle. The hallowed design maxim 'less is more' can sometimes be most relevant to maze design.

In the late twentieth century, a new maze design approach has emerged – the symbolic maze. Unlike stone or turf mazes, symbolism is not merely conveyed in its name or traditional use; the entire maze establishes and then reinforces its symbolism through proportion, imagery and allusion, using traditional and modern techniques wherever appropriate.

In 1969, Michael Ayrton created a maze with ten-foot-high brick walls at Arkville in New York State. The maze contains huge bronze sculptures of the Minotaur, and of Icarus and Daedalus.

Since 1975, Randoll Coate and I, joined latterly by Lesley Beck, as Minotaur Designs, have designed a wide range of symbolic mazes. Built in the grounds of castles, palaces, stately homes, zoos, leisure parks and city centres, they have covered subjects as diverse as heraldic and mythical creatures, an archbishop's sermon, a military victory, a locomotive and a children's wonderland story. The experience of solving each devious puzzle is heightened by discovering its hidden meanings. Innovative concepts such as superimposed layers of imagery, colour mazes, gaze mazes and interactive mazes have been expressed in new forms including brick and stone paths in grass, decorative brick pavement, water, and outdoor and wall mosaic, as well as formal hedges.

The Nature of Puzzlement

A maze is a particular form of puzzle, into which one puts oneself in order to solve it. The evolution of the puzzle maze has been like a game of chess down the centuries between the designer and his public. The difference is that the designer has to play all his moves in advance. Since he must be able to demonstrate a solution, he is ultimately destined to lose the contest.

LIKE ANY ENTERTAINMENT, the maze experience should reach its climax a few minutes before the public have had enough. The ideal time varies by country, location and individual. Unlike most theme park rides, a maze visit does not even have a fixed duration. In Japan, visitors expect a maze to take as long as a feature film or football match, perhaps sixty or ninety minutes or more. At a stately home, thirty or forty minutes would be ideal, whereas in a theme park, less than fifteen minutes might be the average, based on the need to maximize the throughput of visitors each hour. Small children tire more quickly, whilst older children relish the fun and exercise. Young families with pushchairs will sally forth, leaving their older relatives sitting outside to rest and await their return.

Within a given area, the number of junctions also affects the time taken to solve the puzzle. If there are too few junctions, the maze is hardly a challenging puzzle. If there are too many, the area could feel like an orchard, through which it would be easy to proceed. The earliest puzzle mazes had rather too few junctions within their given area for maximum puzzlement.

Maze design is currently going through such a resurgence that any classification is constantly being overtaken by new ideas and innovations. The classification shown in the table simply reflects today's state of the art. In any case, some mazes will defy such fine distinctions. For example, both the Archbishop's Maze and the Bath Festival Maze are multicursal, and yet were designed with a unicursal route through them, using each path once and once only. Many Japanese wooden mazes are both three-dimensional and adjustable.

CLASSIFICATION OF MAZES

Type	
1	Unicursal
2	Processional (quick exit)
3	Simply-connected (goal connected to perimeter)
4	Multiply-connected (goal on central island)
5	Quick three-dimensional exit (just one crossover)
6	Three-dimensional puzzle (bridges and underpasses)
7	Conditional direction (fixed one-way routes)
8	Conditional movement (each move depends on previous one, as in Minotaur Colour Mazes)
9	Adjustable (design changes from day to day)
10	Time-dimensional (design changes every moment)
11	Interactive (design responds to actions of visitors)

PREVIOUS PAGE *The Mirror Maze at Lucerne in Switzerland uses multiple reflections to increase puzzlement.*

OPPOSITE RIGHT *The Archbishop's maze at Grey's Court, Oxfordshire, was laid out in 1981 following the Christian design but with added symbolism (**see p. 116**).*

Unicursal Labyrinths

UNICURSAL MEANS 'ONE-PATHED'. Unicursal labyrinths have no junctions, but consist of a single path leading from the entrance to the goal. There are three main forms of unicursal labyrinth: Classical, Roman and medieval Christian. All three forms share a hidden characteristic, internal rotational symmetry.

The archetypal unicursal labyrinth is the Classical seven-ring design. To construct it, start with a cross and four points. Then join each line of the cross to its respective point. This can be done to any scale, with a wide range of materials.

The Classical seven-ring labyrinth. Start with a cross and four points. Then join each line of the cross to its respective point.

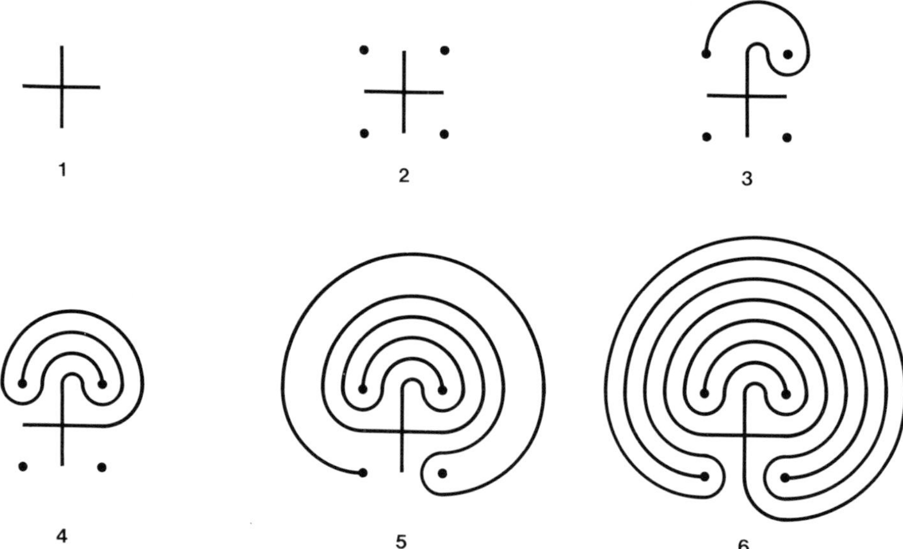

This simplicity of construction, and its satisfying result, makes the Classical labyrinth a very easy design to mark out without measuring equipment. This helps explain its widespread use over thousands of years.

The eight barriers are counterpart to the seven paths they enclose, so this design can also be shown in terms of its seven pathways. Then, by cutting the design from the entrance to its goal, and gradually folding it out, the same design can be portrayed as a rectangle. The highest horizontal line represents the first outer path ring, and the lowest line represents the seventh inner path ring.

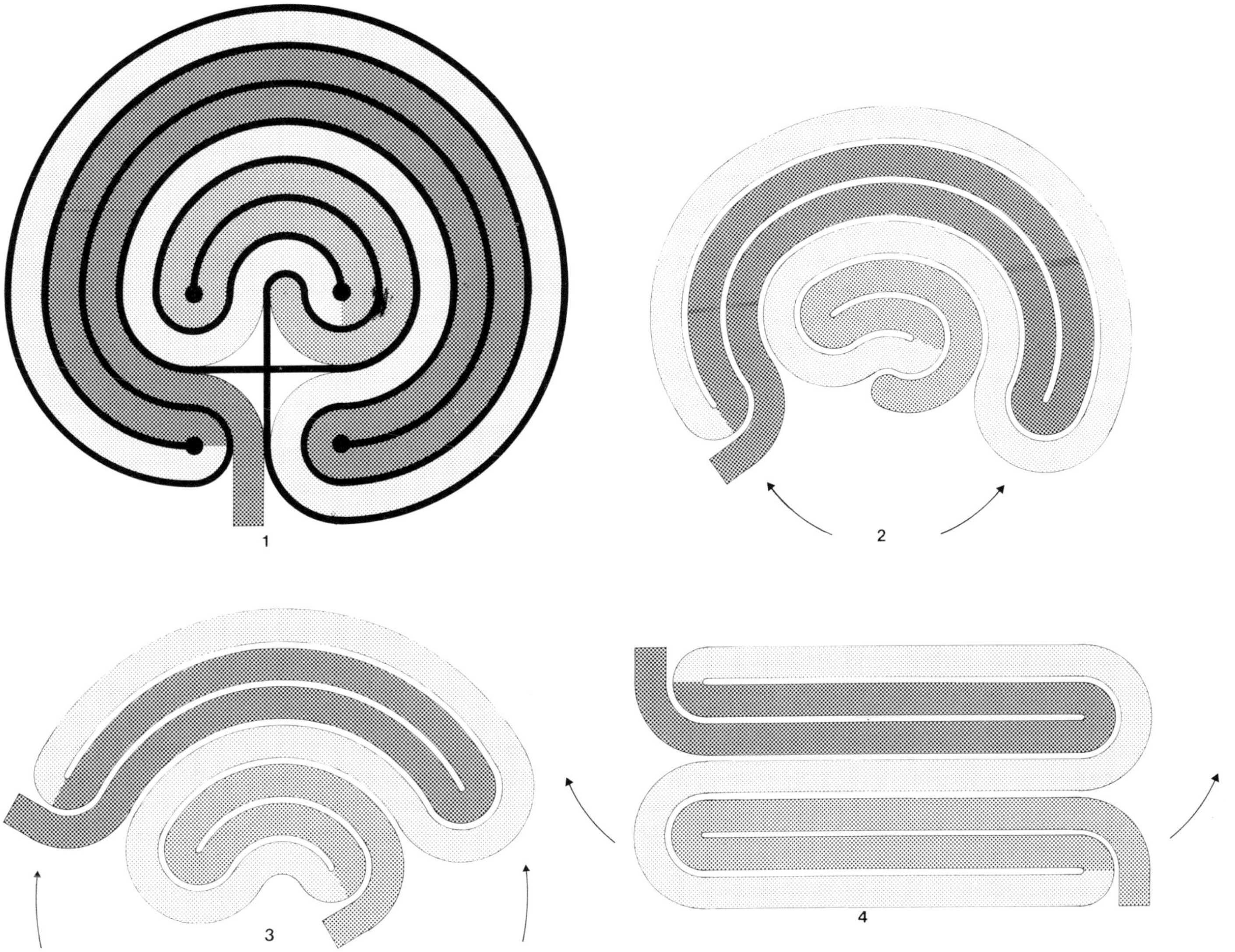

Topological transformation of the Classical seven-ring labyrinth. Make a vertical cut, and then fold the design out into a rectangle.

The internal rotational symmetry of the design now becomes apparent, as can be demonstrated by rotating the design 180 degrees.

When first seeing a labyrinth, this internal rotational symmetry is not at all obvious. However, this hidden symmetry can be demonstrated in all three forms of unicursal labyrinth.

There are many variations of the Classical seven-ring design. For example, the number of rings of paths can be increased in multiples of four, to produce designs with eleven or fifteen rings of paths.

The second unicursal form is the Roman labyrinth design. It was usually

LEFT OPPOSITE *The Classical labyrinth design at Somerton, expanded to fifteen rings of paths, contained within sixteen divisions.*

created square or circular, for the practical reason that it was laid in mosaic to cover a square floor. Roman mosaic labyrinths first appeared before the birth of Christ; their cruciform shape had nothing to do with Christian symbolism.

Unfolded in the same way, its internal rotational symmetry is revealed. Each quarter of its design resembles the pattern of a complete Classical labyrinth, producing a somewhat repetitive path. However, these narrow mosaic maze paths were not intended for walking along; rather, they were a border decoration, and perhaps a maze to follow with the eye. At the centre, a vigorous mosaic representation of Theseus slaying the Minotaur might provide artistic justification for the labyrinthine border.

RIGHT *Transformation of the Roman labyrinth, showing the same pattern repeated in each of its four quarters.*

ABOVE *The stone pavement maze laid within the nave of Chartres Cathedral.*

The third unicursal form is the medieval Christian maze. Its earliest appearance is in a document dated AD 860–62 in the Vatican Library. Although the stimulus for the design may have come from contact with the Arab world, with its ideas, geometry and mathematics, no evidence of a labyrinth has yet been found there.

The Chartres maze is the oldest surviving medieval Christian maze built full size. Still the most celebrated example, it is laid in blue and white marble in the nave of the cathedral. The Chartres maze has a remarkable relationship with the great west rose window, above the cathedral's west door. Both are the same shape, both are the same size, and the maze is exactly as far from the west door as the rose window is above it. Thus if the rose window were folded down, it would exactly cover the maze. The same topological transformation method reveals a quite different internal symmetry.

Progress along the path is far less inhibited than in the Roman pattern, with generous clockwise and anticlockwise sweeps right round the design, both early on and towards the end.

The medieval Christian maze design was a fundamental breakthrough. It brought freshness to the pilgrimage journey it represented, complementing the brilliant stained glass light from the rose windows above. The gothic cathedrals abounded with innovation. Soaring gothic arches and light flying

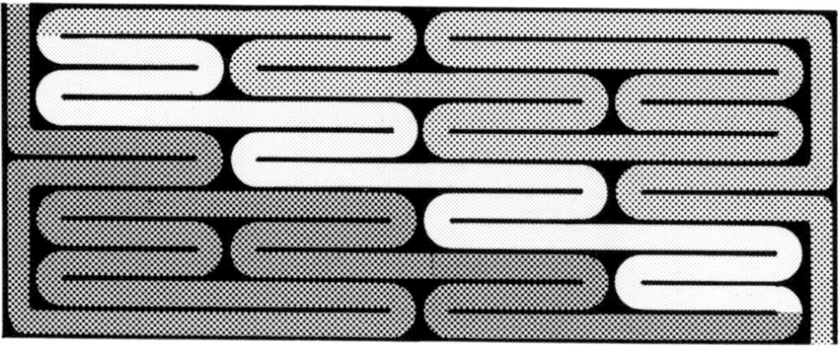

The transformation sequence of the medieval Christian maze. The paths sweep exuberantly right round the design.

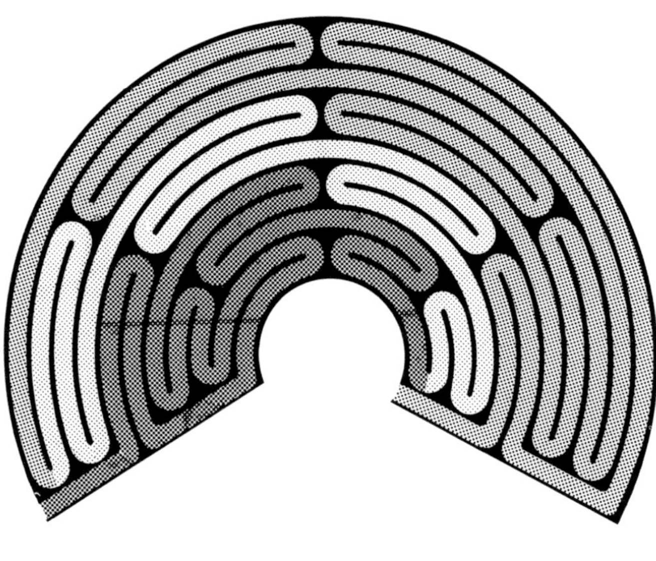

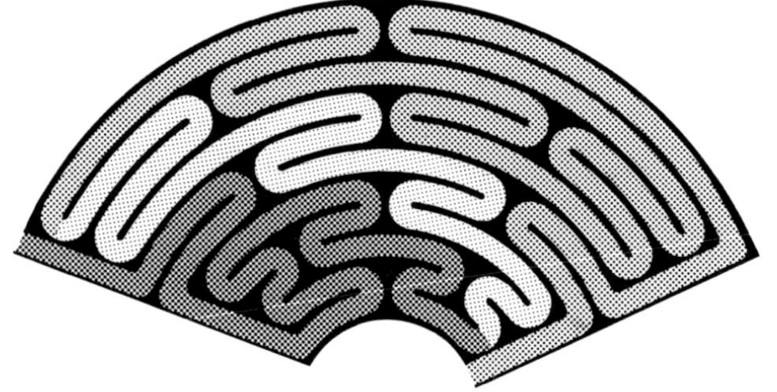

buttresses replaced heavy Norman arches, that after a thousand years had failed to improve on the functional semicircular Roman arches.

As a path reaches an axis, it has a choice of three ways forward: to continue on the same ring, to double back one ring inwards, or to double back one ring outwards. Curiously, this has exact parallels with change-ringing, an art which originated in cathedrals, whereby a bell in position n can only reach n, $n+1$ or $n-1$ in the subsequent change.

The medieval Christian maze is found in two shapes, circular and octagonal. The more obvious square shape was never used in European cathedrals, which raises several questions. Perhaps the square was avoided, due to the pagan or Bacchanalian connotations of Roman mosaic labyrinths, or perhaps the circular and octagonal forms were positively selected for their symbolism. This was, after all, the heyday of masonic knowledge within a trade guild, when such knowledge was used less for social advantage, and more to solve the practical problems of making the cathedrals stay up.

Octagonal medieval Christian pavement maze at Amiens. The distinctive pattern of the Maltese Cross emerges from the design.

The catalyst for the innovations of the gothic Cathedrals was probably contact with the Arab world during the Crusades. Mathematics, numerals and the concept of zero were crucial for accurate calculation, to replace trial and error. Precise calculation would have been essential to conceive the elegant dimensions of flying buttresses. With knights returning from the Crusades, wanting to build their new Jerusalems, pavement labyrinths offered another opportunity to incorporate their secret symbolism.

The two main orders of chivalry were the Knights Templar, and the Knights of St John. When the Knights Templar reached Jerusalem, there was no longer any purpose in their churches facing east towards the Holy Land, so they built them circular. Circular Templar churches can be found to this day in London, Cambridge and elsewhere and it is possible that the circular labyrinths were created by the Knights Templar. The emblem of the Knights of St John was a

ABOVE *The pavement maze at St Omer.*

LEFT *The Reverend Paul Lucas, former Vicar of Batheaston, had a great fascination with the pavement maze of St Omer. When the floor of the south transept required replacing, he took the opportunity to lay out a stone pavement labyrinth, and personally got down on his knees and created this remarkable pavement maze.*

OPPOSITE TOP RIGHT *The design of the turf maze, formerly at Pimperne.*

OPPOSITE RIGHT *The pavement maze in Ely Cathedral installed by Giles Gilbert Scott as part of his restoration works in the nineteenth century.*

black cross on a white background (the Maltese Cross), meeting at a point at its centre. This emblem produces eight wedge-shaped divisions, and can be discerned in the octagonal form of the medieval Christian maze.

Apart from the three pure forms of unicursal labyrinth, there have been many other unicursal variations, but none have truly concentric rings of paths. Variations include the less compact Christian form at St Omer, and its modern copy in Batheaston church. There was formerly a fascinating meandering maze at Pimperne.

Sir Gilbert Scott's restoration of Ely Cathedral in 1870 included a stone pavement labyrinth under the West Tower. He was clearly influenced by the pavement mazes in the cathedrals of Northern France, and wished to echo their character. Moreover, rather than making a slavish imitation of any particular maze, he decided to produce an innovative design of his own, whose

path length is the same as the height of the tower above it. Seen from the south-west corner of the design, a cruciform image is apparent. Intriguingly, he was unaware or chose not to observe the medieval Christian practice of internal rotational symmetry. As a result, the path through the maze to its goal does not contain the regular rhythms so characteristic of medieval Christian mazes. In the 1970s the Ely design was precisely copied and laid out in the porch of the cathedral in Pietermaritzburg, South Africa. Here there is neither internal rotational symmetry nor any significance to the path length.

The processional labyrinth is almost but not quite unicursal. Its additional short exit path from the goal, out of the maze, is of great significance. This short exit makes it possible for a procession of any length to pass through the maze, without congestion at the goal. Such labyrinths could therefore have a significant role in the life of the community, as everyone could take part together, unlike other unicursal labyrinths, where only one or a few could tread it at once. In a processional labyrinth, the great majority of the path occurs whilst approaching the goal. The demands of geometry result in a characteristic kidney shape, and such patterns are found in Germany and Poland.

The ancient turf maze at Hanover.

Puzzle Mazes

PUZZLE MAZES EVOLVED in a surprisingly haphazard way. Although the concept of the unicursal labyrinth remained unquestioned, successive generations portrayed it in a wide range of materials. From their earliest origins until the Middle Ages, labyrinths were invariably unicursal – from the earliest rock carvings, early coinage and Roman mosaic, to Scandinavian paths between boulders, German turf paths and French cathedral pavements. They could always be seen at a glance in their entirety, and therefore could not conceal any junctions or choices. Nor was there any reason to wish to create a puzzle, since the labyrinth evolved from a path to be followed by the eye or finger, to a processional path to be ritually walked by the local community.

Early gardening introduced the use of vertical shrubs and hedges between the paths. For the first time, the maze design was hidden, and it would be possible to create extra puzzlement by concealing a succession of junctions and choices out of sight of each other. Yet the earliest garden mazes with low or tall hedges did not take advantage of this opportunity. In England, France and the Netherlands, block-type mazes were created, which were convoluted paths cut into large areas of hedge. The width of the hedges was not uniformly narrow, which was later to become imperative in the quest for packing the maximum maze puzzle into the minimum area. This suggests that block-type mazes derive their origin from parterre design, where the patterns rejoiced in dilating and blossoming into elaborate, geometric and non-linear shapes.

Block-type hedge mazes were portrayed in many of the illustrations by Kip, Knyff and others, including the mazes at Belvoir Castle, Boughton, Exton Park and Trinity College, Oxford. The hedge maze formerly at Theobalds in Hertfordshire provides another intriguing clue to this transitional period. At first glance it seems like a typical puzzle hedge maze, complete with uniformly narrow hedges. However, closer inspection shows it has no junctions at all, and its design is derived from the medieval Christian pattern.

Plan of the former maze at Theobalds in Hertfordshire, derived from the medieval Christian pattern and without junctions.

Eventually the opportunity for deception within hedge mazes was realized, and after thousands of years of unicursal labyrinths, hedge mazes began to offer junctions and choices for the first time. The Hampton Court Maze is a good example of the earliest form of puzzle maze. Junctions lead off to dead ends to both left and right, and the main path is not made clear in any way. The alleyways contain twists and turns, both large and small, and further disorientation is achieved by the different angles within its trapezoid shape. However, perceptive visitors gradually noticed that this kind of maze could always be solved using the 'hand-on-wall' method – that is, by keeping consistently to the left, in and out of each dead end. Whenever this method works to the left, it will always work to the right as well. This is caused by the

Simply-connected Puzzle Mazes

The simply-connected maze at Hampton Court. Using the hand-on-wall method, medium-shaded walls would be used by the right hand, and dark-shaded walls by the left hand. The light-shaded hedge indicates an 'island' – an innovative idea, whose significance and potential was not appreciated at the time. Notice the tell-tale strip of hedge, with different shading on its two sides, connecting the goal's hedge with the perimeter hedge. This betrays the maze as being simply-connected.

fact that the hedge which surrounds the goal is continuously connected to the perimeter hedge. This topological characteristic provides our definition of the next maze type – the simply-connected maze.

Simply-connected mazes continue to be built to the present day, despite modern design techniques whch overcome this fundamental weakness. This is partly due to the reputation of the Hampton Court Maze, of which more than a dozen copies have been created, as far apart as England, America and Australia. Occasionally, simply-connected mazes are consciously designed, due to other design considerations, such as in the Archbishop's Maze and the Bath Festival Maze. But the great majority of simply-connected mazes have been created in ignorance of the wider possibilities.

Multiply-connected Puzzle Mazes

The second Earl Stanhope, an eminent mathematician, designed at least three mazes, including that at Chevening in Kent. This maze, built in the 1820s, was the first to have 'islands' to overcome the hand-on-wall solving method. When applying this method, one simply goes round the edge of the maze and returns to the entrance. The maze design achieves this by detaching the perimeter hedge from the hedge surrounding the goal. Thus the goal is located within a central 'island'. For added puzzlement, there are also a number of other 'minor islands' within the design. These minor islands could be removed without making much difference to the puzzle.

The detachment of the perimeter barrier from the barrier surrounding the goal provides the definition for the multiply-connected maze. Topologically, no further elaboration than this can be added to a two-dimensional static monochrome puzzle maze. Earl Stanhope, however, displayed one further refinement in the Chevening design. He effectively spurned the use of dead-ends, so visitors do not experience the rejection of reaching a dead-end and having to retrace their steps. This can give a wonderful and yet spurious sense of elation and progress. Since passages often appear quite different walked in opposite directions, the elimination of dead-ends makes the maze seem more extensive and puzzling.

LEFT OPPOSITE *The labyrinthine hedges at La Gaude in Provence do not form a true hedge maze, although in character it echoes the style of the early block-type maze.*

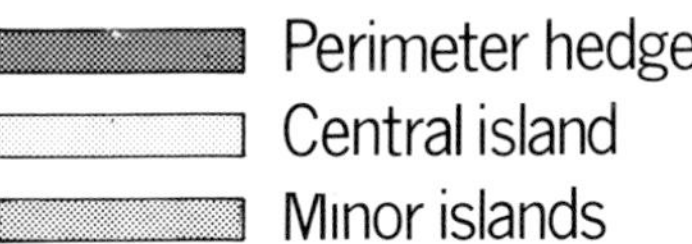

The multiply-connected maze at Chevening. The heavy-shaded walls are the perimeter hedge, and the light-shaded walls surround the goal. The medium-shaded hedges indicate 'islands' within the design.

Three-Dimensional Puzzle Mazes

Two-dimensional hedge mazes usually oblige visitors to retrace their steps back through the puzzle maze to the entrance. This makes the most of a small maze. However, after the climax of reaching the goal, visitors may spend nearly as much time finding their way out. A quick exit keeps up the elation of having solved the maze. In some ways, a well-designed maze experience has parallels with a theme park ride: entering, assimilating, exploring, deducing, solving, reaching the goal, and then leaving.

A third dimension is needed if the maze is to have a quick exit and yet remain multiply-connected. Only one crossover is needed, either using a bridge or a tunnel. Tunnels are comparatively rare, being much more expensive than bridges. However, an underground tunnel is a superb form of deception, since visitors in the maze above can remain completely unaware of its existence until the end. A tunnel offers great scope for special effects, since there can be complete control over light, sound, texture, humidity and even

The Chevening Maze in Kent (maze not open to the public)

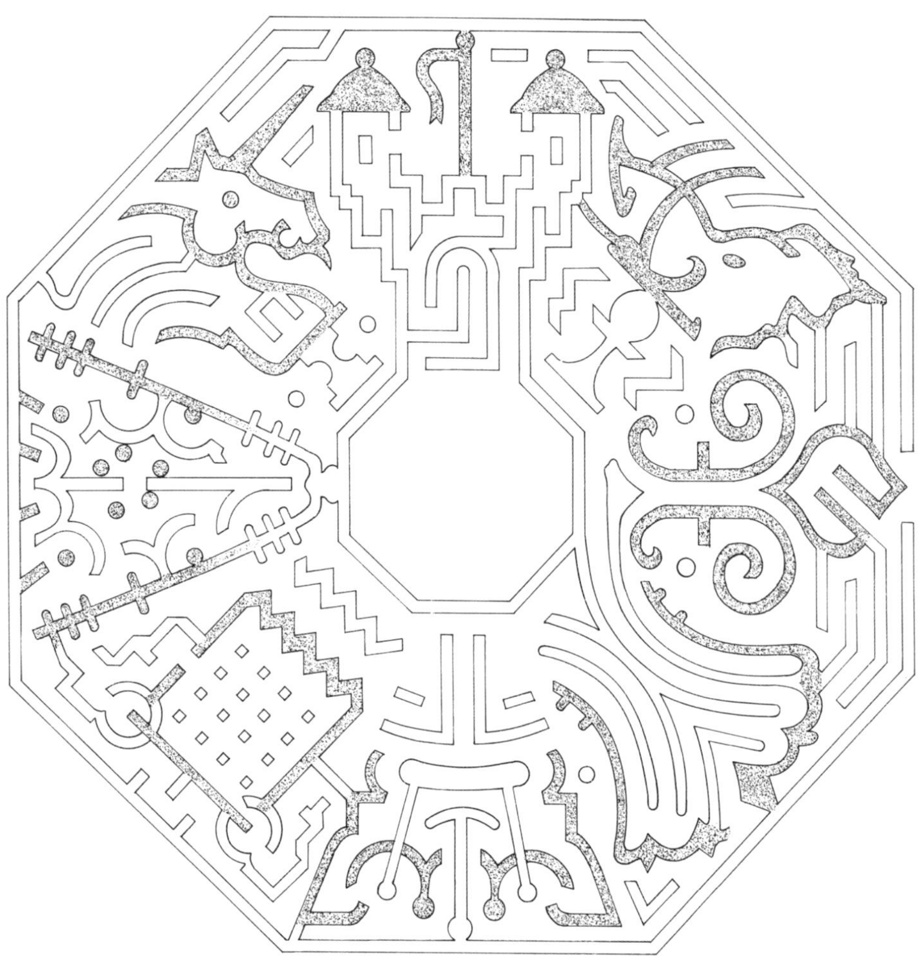

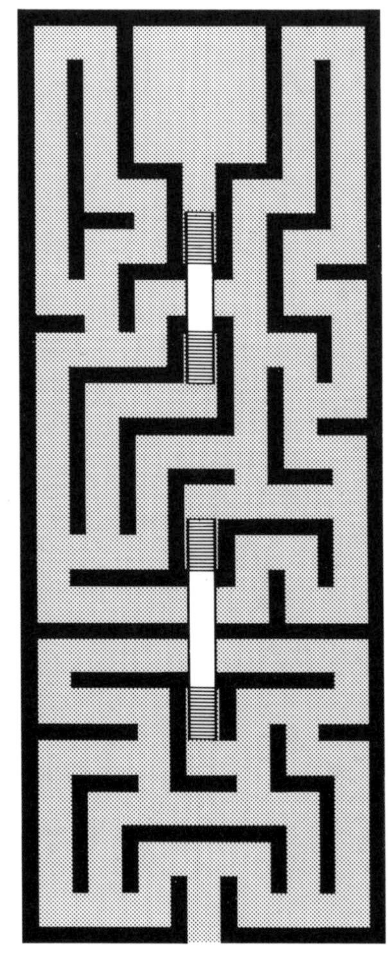

fragrance. The Leeds Castle Maze contains probably the world's finest exit tunnel of any maze.

A single bridge can also provide a quick exit. It is less expensive than a tunnel, and has the added advantage of offering a raised viewpoint for visitors. The Alice-in-Wonderland Maze at Merritown House has one wooden bridge, which also forms a gateway over the entrance and exit paths. The maze puzzle is multiply-connected, since one can go round and round the maze without reaching the goal. After solving the maze, there is a quick exit path.

Provided enough bridges are used, any fully three-dimensional maze puzzle can be represented on a two-dimensional surface, such as the landscape. The Longleat Maze designed by Greg Bright contains several innovations, including deceptively similar spiral junctions, and elongated forks to persuade visitors to 'conserve their momentum' instead of making a hairpin turn. It has

ABOVE *The puzzle opportunities of a fully three-dimensional maze, with a series of 'frying pans'. This hypothetical maze is analysed for its topological structure.*

The Roxburghe Maze, formerly at Floors Castle, with a quick exit but no bridge or tunnel. As a result it is simply-connected, with the perimeter hedge connected to the goal, and can be solved using the hand-on-wall method.

The superb subterranean grotto at the centre of the Leeds Castle Maze designed by Vernon Gibberd. Descending still further, a ninety foot tunnel leads to the exit, well below the paths and hedges of the maze above.

The Alice-in-Wonderland Maze, with a quick exit passing under a bridge.

six wooden bridges, with paths sometimes crossing over more than one other path. Visitors first enter a topological 'frying pan', whose sides are unscalable; walking round its perimeter using the hand-on-wall method takes them straight back to the entrance. The only way out is by taking a bridge which rises over the rim of the pan, and into the next part of the maze.

A three-dimensional maze may have a series of 'frying pans' before reaching the goal. Where this occurs, different sides of a hedge or barrier have different topological 'colours' (unlike a two-dimensional maze, where both sides of every hedge or island are always the same colour).

Conditional Direction Mazes

One-way maze paths can add to the puzzle. These vary from herringbone patterns in brick paths, one-way doors or other barriers activated by breaking a beam or pushing a button or escape bar, to rotating steel gates, as used to let visitors out of zoos. Rotating steel gates are used within some Japanese wooden mazes, to prevent visitors going back the way they came.

Conditional Movement Mazes

For further variety, each move can depend on the previous one. Thus the choice available at each junction will depend on how you approach it. This concept was foreseen in literature, long before it was ever presented in reality. Jorges Luis Borges, in his fictional story 'The Garden of Forking Paths' within his book *Labyrinths*, wrote of a spy, Yu Tsun whose duty compels him to seek out a certain Stephen Albert. To Yu Tsun's astonishment, he finds that Albert is a learned Sinologist, and had closely studied the writings of his ancestor, Ts'ui Pen. The text included the words 'I leave to the various futures (not to all) my garden of forking paths'. Yu Tsun is overjoyed as they talk of so much they share in common, yet simultaneously deeply sorrowful. Prophetically, Albert murmurs 'Time forks perpetually towards innumerable futures. In one of them I am your enemy.' Yu Tsun replies, 'The future already exists' and reluctantly shoots him dead, just as an officer approaches to arrest him. Yu Tsun's task had been to communicate the name of a city called Albert, and the only way he could find to do this was to kill a man of that name, so that it would be reported in the wartime newspapers. Duty and a stronger, older loyalty had overruled their newly-discovered friendship, and Yu Tsun ends by expressing his unutterable contrition and weariness. This course of action was only necessary because of the circumstances in which the encounter took place. If preceding events had been different, the same encounter could have been entirely one of friendship.

Colour mazes provide the extra puzzle dimension required. All unicursal and multicursal mazes mentioned so far have been 'monochrome', in the sense that all their paths are treated in an identical way. The use of colour can be literal, with paths actually coloured differently, or diagrammatic, with different surface textures or patterns. The colours can even be a computer system shorthand for the way movement is permitted around the maze, with visitors initially unaware of the reasons why certain choices become available.

'Edward's Enigma' colour maze in the garden of the puzzle collector Edward Hordern.

The wooden puzzle maze at Kyoto, in Japan. The bridges create a fully three-dimensional puzzle, linking the checkpoint towers in the four corners.

Various designers have devised mazes using colour in one way or another. Greg Bright painted a colour maze on a twelve foot canvas, with elaborate instructions to follow. Seymour Robins' delightful 'Bees' colour maze has passed the ultimate consumer test, by effectively distracting the attention of children in the local dental surgery in New England – it is pinned to the ceiling directly above the dentist's chair.

Minotaur colour mazes are created in various materials, including coloured brick paving, coloured bridges between islands in a lake, and portable mazes of brightly coloured squares. In these colour mazes, the choice of path depends

on the colour of the previous path. During each maze attempt, a single rule is followed. Sometimes the same colour maze can be attempted several times, each time obeying a different rule. All these mazes have coloured paths that run from one node to another without changing colour, with the nodes themselves neutrally coloured.

Adjustable Mazes

The wooden walls of Japanese mazes can be adjusted from day to day, to overcome design weaknesses, and to provide a different puzzle each week for regular visitors. During any one visit, however, the maze design is static.

Time-dimensional Mazes

The design of a time-dimensional maze changes from moment to moment whilst visitors are inside it. This is achieved by gates or barriers which open and close at different times. Time becomes an extra dimension to the maze. However, unlike other dimensions, time cannot be retraced, and this provides extra puzzle design scope.

Interactive Mazes

Interactive mazes not only change their design in real time, but also respond to the actions of visitors. The results can vary from barriers opening and the maze design changing, to special music, sound or lighting effects. Effects can be hauntingly beautiful, especially if music or fountains, for example, respond simultaneously to one's actions.

Further Types of Puzzle Maze

The usual way of using a maze is for one person to enter it, and search for the goal until he finds it. But there can be other ways of using a maze, for example by leading a procession, which must achieve certain objectives in a given order, without the procession crossing over itself. The Labyrinth at Versailles involved passing thirty-nine statues in the correct order, without repeating one's path. In the Maze of the Mysteries of the Gospels at Wyck Rissington, an annual procession went past fifteen points without crossing over itself.

Human ingenuity is likely to produce a continued proliferation of types of maze. Yet beyond a certain point, considerations of appearance, atmosphere and meaning overtake mere puzzlement. Like ice skating, mazes should be judged as much on artistic impression as technical merit. The design judgement needed to combine these two strands makes the art of maze making so fascinating, and its future so exciting.

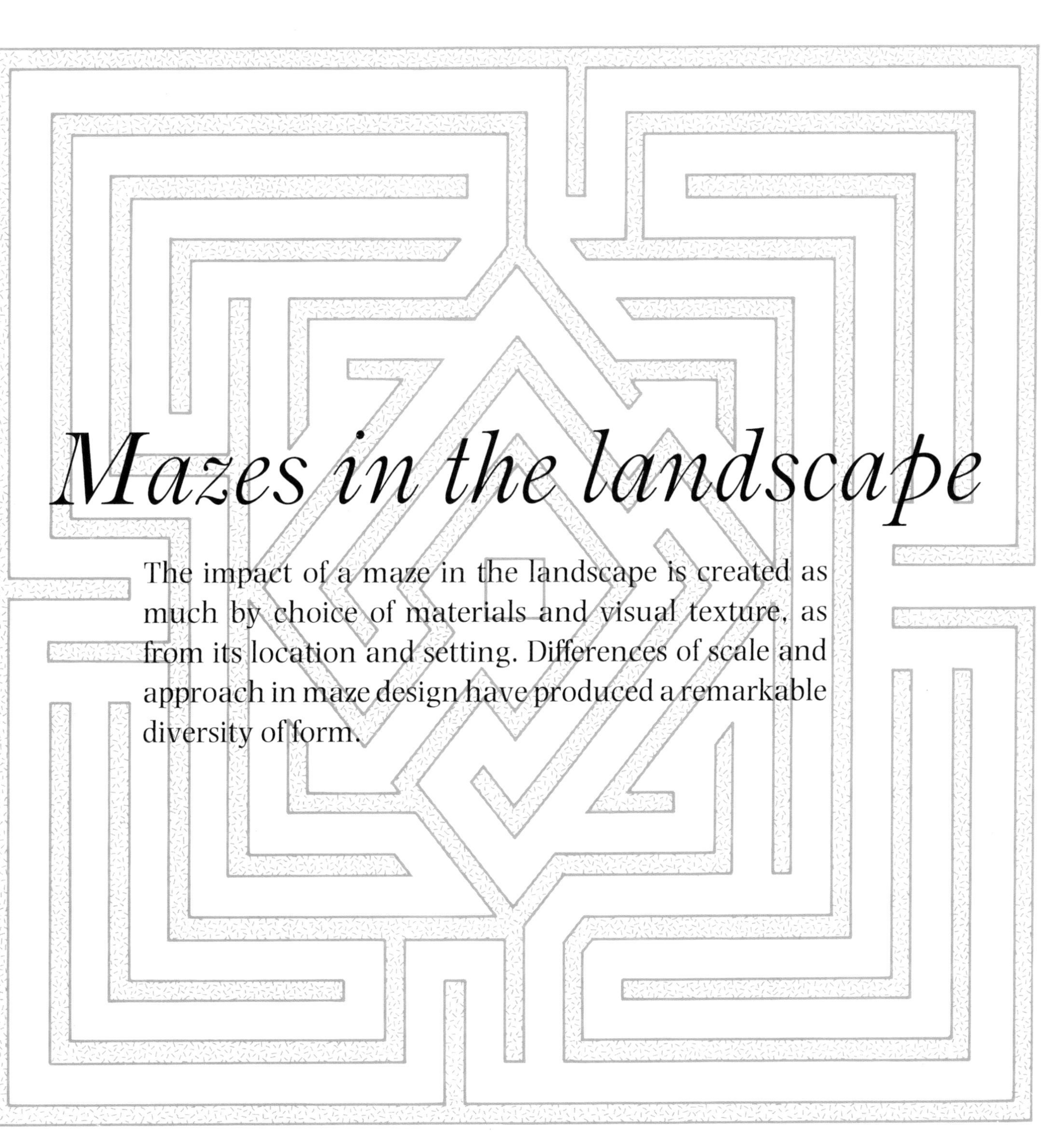

Mazes in the landscape

The impact of a maze in the landscape is created as much by choice of materials and visual texture, as from its location and setting. Differences of scale and approach in maze design have produced a remarkable diversity of form.

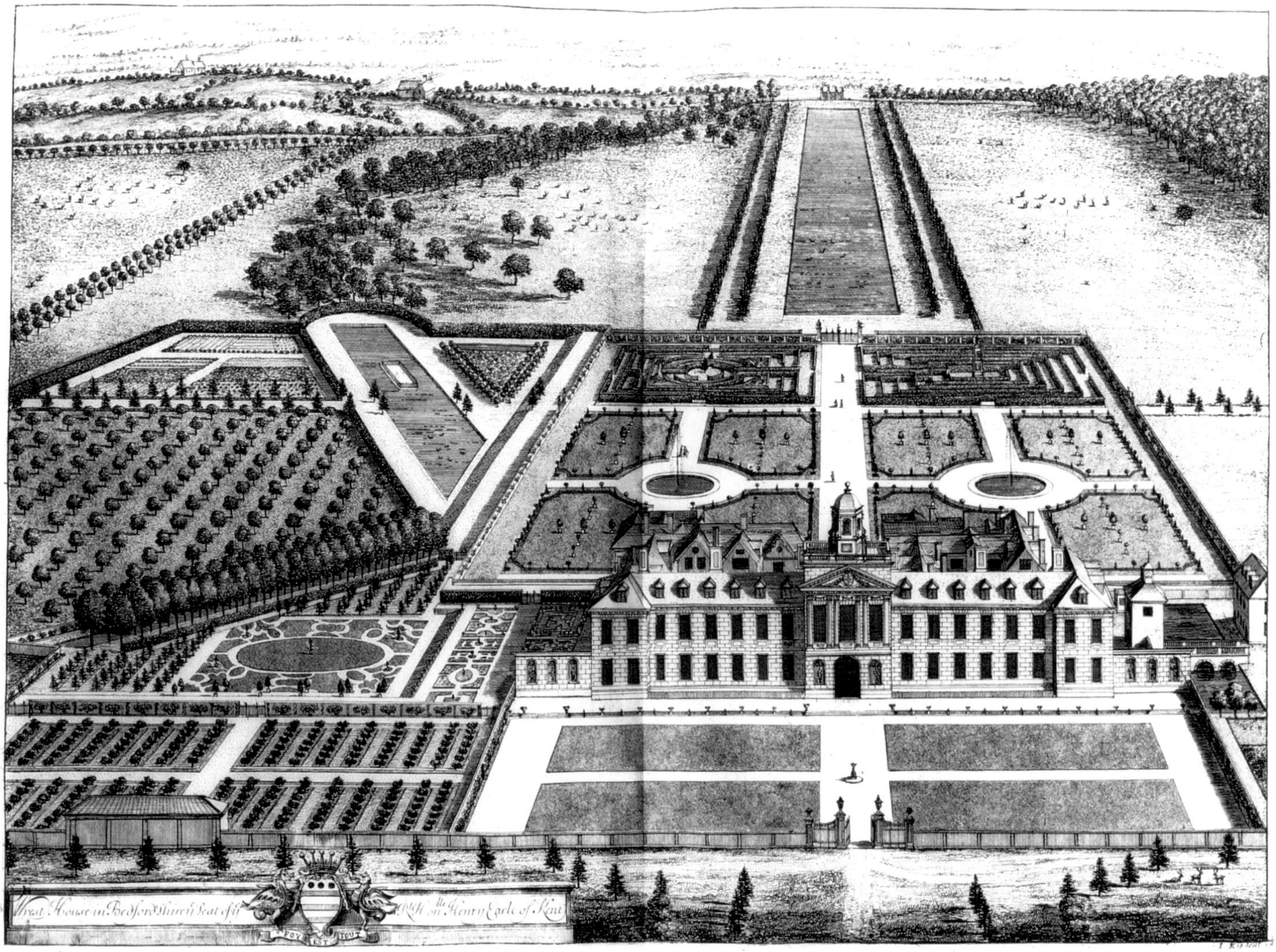

ABOVE *Kip's engraving of Wrest House, Bedfordshire, reveals not one but two hedge mazes within the formal gardens. Both are situated so they can be clearly seen from the windows of the house, creating a natural destination for a gentle stroll.*

PREVIOUS PAGE *This maze at Egeskov on Fyn Island, dating back to the seventeenth century, and set in a fairy-tale location, is only one of two in the grounds. A second larger maze was planted in bamboo in 1988.*

THE LOCATION OF a maze within the landscape often reveals a great deal about its origin and purpose. Decorative mazes, whether cut in rock, carved on a church pillar, made in stained glass or laid out as mosaic, are not solved by walking. Instead, they are intended to be followed by the eye, or traced with a finger. The Bath maze contains seven 'gaze' mazes in mosaic, at the centre of a full-size path maze.

A maze on common land or in a public place is available for use by the whole community – whether as a turf maze on a village green, a stone labyrinth on the coast, or a modern maze in a city centre or public park. The earliest hedge mazes were in the gardens of kings and princes. These gardens would not have been private in our modern understanding of the concept – indeed a feudal king could not expect privacy even in his own bedchamber, since all and sundry had the right of access to him at all times.

Hedge mazes were not usually planted immediately beside the house. Here,

formal designs on a smaller scale would be more suitable, and parterres and knot gardens were often laid out, to be appreciated from upper windows overlooking the area. The intricate scale of pavement mazes allows them close to buildings, sometimes actually within Tudor courtyards, as at Temple Newsam House near Leeds and Kentwell Hall in Suffolk. Some of the earliest pavement mazes for walking around are inside medieval cathedrals.

Early hedge mazes were, however, usually within sight of the house or palace, strongly reinforcing the architectural formality of the building, as well as the wealth and power of its owner. This relationship between house and maze can still be seen at Hatfield House, an Elizabethan royal palace, where the rectangular hedge maze acts like a mirror in the landscape, reflecting the formality of the house across the rose gardens in between.

CHENIES MANOR MAZE

The portrait dated 1573 of Edward Lord Russell, whose family owned Chenies Manor, showing a maze in the background.

John Russell, later first earl of Bedford, acquired Chenies Manor House by marriage in the sixteenth century. A portrait of his grandson, dated 1573, now hanging at Woburn Abbey, shows a turf maze in the background with, presumably, the sitter, Edward, Lord Russell, standing at its centre. The motto beneath the maze cameo, FATA VIAM INVENIENT (or, the Fates find a Way), suggests that the figure at the heart of the maze is intended to symbolize triumph over adversity. The detail of the maze design was almost certainly depicted incorrectly by the painter, as its paths do not line up properly at the top, and thus appear to form a spiral. Nevertheless, in the spirit of authenticity, in 1983 Denys Tweddell faithfully recreated its spiral design at Chenies Manor within a fifty foot diameter. A rope was wound around a circle of stakes and its end marked the course of the spirals as the rope unwound. The result is uncanny

The turf and gravel maze at Chenies Manor laid out in 1983 following the rather curious design in the portrait.

The maze at Greys Court, conceived by Lady Brunner.

after seeing the portrait first. Whether the maze in the portrait was based on an actual maze at Chenies or is purely allegorical, it certainly places the idea of the maze or labyrinth squarely within the terms of everyday reference of Elizabethan England.

A garden maze can also act like a magnet in the landscape, drawing its visitors through intervening gardens before reaching the maze itself. The visit to the maze becomes a structured excursion, firstly approaching through the immediate gardens, then walking within the maze, thirdly enjoying the delights at its goal, and finally returning by a different route through the gardens. This was Lady Brunner's specific idea at Greys Court. The same principle was applied at Versailles and Chantilly, and can still be seen at Hampton Court Palace and Chatsworth.

In the twentieth century, Disneyland has pioneered similar structured excursions within its fantasy rides. The ride itself is the experience, but to handle the crowds, queuing is inevitable. This problem is turned into an opportunity, with lines of visitors constantly on the move, passing through one themed area after another, building up their anticipation.

Modern mazes in their turn almost seem to imitate theme park rides. Wooden mazes in Japan have a sequence of objectives to reach; the visitor

EXIT

accumulates a series of stamps on his card, before reaching a puzzle shop at the end. The Leeds Castle Maze involves entering, solving, reaching a high viewpoint, descending into a wonderful grotto, and leaving by way of a themed exit tunnel. Mazes have a great advantage over all other forms of ride – there is no need to queue up in line outside, and all the time is spent inside enjoying the maze. Moreover, unlike the passivity of theme park rides, maze visitors actively make choices, and are in control of their progress.

Some mazes are not so much a supporting garden feature, as the entire purpose of the location. Mazes as stand-alone attractions flourish as far apart as Wanaka in New Zealand and Symonds Yat in England. Many wooden mazes in Japan are a destination in their own right, rather than part of a greater landscape. The WOOZ maze at Vacaville in California is a multi-million dollar development, complete with its own restaurant.

The recent hedge maze, planted in the former walled garden at Cawdor Castle, derived its design from the ancient Roman mosaic at Coimbra in Portugal. The maze has a single path leading all the way to the goal.

Garden Hedge Mazes

THE TAMING OF the wild woods of Europe over the centuries was marked by forest clearance, settlement, enclosures and walled gardens. The pleasure gardens of great houses and castles came nearest to paradise and perfection on earth. In these enchanted gardens, the living hedge maze was the ultimate outdoor plaything, and in Europe, it is still widely regarded as a supreme expression of the maze as an art-form. The earliest hedge mazes were

LEFT OPPOSITE *The maze at Vacaville, USA, is three-dimensional, the bridges allowing an overview before descending into the puzzle once more.*

LEFT *The Glendurgan maze, created by Alfred Fox in 1833, is one of Britain's earliest surviving hedge mazes. It is one of three mazes owned by the National Trust, the other two being at Greys Court and Tatton Park. The free-flowing design was a highly innovative departure from formal patterns, as was its inspired positioning on one side of the narrow valley, giving an almost bird's eye view of its sinuous laurel hedges from the opposite side.*

LEFT *America's most famous hedge maze is in the gardens of the Governor's Palace at colonial Williamsburg, Virginia. It was planted in 1935. The design is based on the Hampton Court Maze, at about half the size.*

ABOVE AND LEFT *The only entrance to and exit from the Russborough Maze in Co. Wicklow is through the eighteenth-century riding school. The design of this formal hedge maze, planted in 1989, conceals a clue to the identity of its owner, for Sir Alfred Beit's family were early pioneers in the world diamond industry. A statue of cupid stands on a column at the centre, tantalisingly indicating the goal from all parts of the maze.*

OVERLEAF *The Chatsworth maze, planted in 1962 to an earlier design, occupies the former site of Paxton's Great Stove glasshouse. The maze is surrounded by mature wellingtonias, with stone bridges at each end of the garden.*

comparatively simple puzzles, yet created on a scale which provided a quarter of an hour's diversion in a private garden. They were a light-hearted playing place for children, child-minded adults and courting couples.

European hedge mazes are intended for permanence. They can take five to ten years to reach maturity, a long time in anyone's lifespan, although, as one Duke remarked, 'What's six years? – our family has been here for four centuries'. The locations of hedge mazes are carefully chosen within the landscape, and the full range of landscape features can be lavished upon them – seating and sundials, statues and fountains, towers and bridges, even grottoes and underground tunnels. Relatively slow-growing hedge materials are best, as they hold their shape well and only require one major clipping each year. Yew provides formality, maintains a precise shape and is long-lived. Beech creates a lighter dappled atmosphere, and hornbeam and holly grow steadily and strongly. Other materials may be suitable, for reasons of soil, drainage, climate, geography, immediate surroundings or other considerations. The careful choice of plant material also plays an important part in establishing the character of a maze, and its artistic impression within the landscape. Because of the bulky width of the hedges, there is often room for only fifteen to twenty rows of hedges across the design. This can present a considerable design challenge, with conciseness of design at a premium. Most puzzle hedge mazes are solved within thirty minutes.

The hedge maze at Hampton Court Palace.

HAMPTON COURT MAZE

Hampton Court Palace has probably the world's most famous hedge maze, the oldest in England. It was planted as part of the gardens laid out for William of Orange in 1690, by George London and Henry Wise. Its unusual trapezoid shape is explained by the plan of the Wilderness, where the shape of the maze is dictated by two diagonal paths and a further curving path. This helps date the maze since clearly the maze could not have been planted prior to the layout of the Wilderness.

The maze faced its greatest challenge early on, when Capability Brown became the Royal Gardener, and for twenty years lived in the house alongside the maze. Brown's reputation had been built on sweeping away some two hundred fine gardens all over the country, but the king expressly ordered Brown not to interfere with the Hampton Court maze, and thus it survived.

The maze was described in Jerome K. Jerome's *Three Men in a Boat*, and this novel established in many minds the connection between mazes, blazers and straw boater hats. In Victorian times, this maze design was copied over a dozen times, both in Britain as well as in North America and Australia. Such was its reputation that others were keen to emulate it when creating a hedge maze elsewhere. To this day, the Hampton Court maze remains in many ways synonymous with hedge mazes throughout the English speaking world.

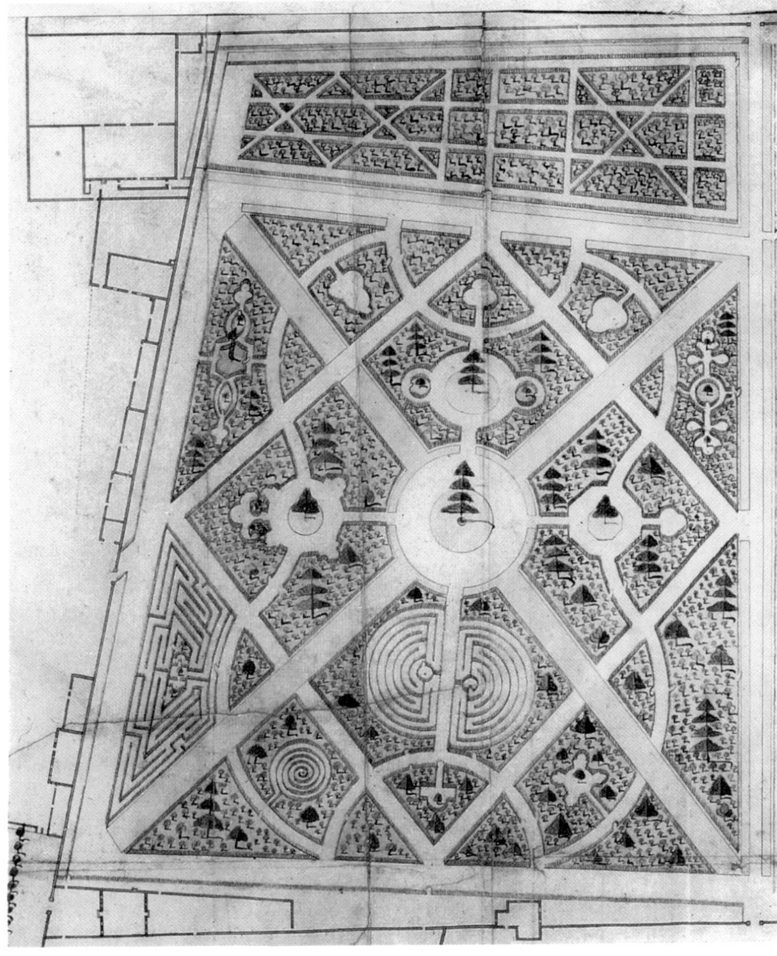

Plan of the Wilderness, showing the trapezoid shape formed by intersecting paths, which gives the Hampton Court maze its distinctive shape.

'PYRAMID', CHÂTEAU DE BELOEIL

The hedges of the beech maze at the Château de Beloeil, Belgium's stateliest home, are being trained to grow as an angled pyramid, with its tallest rows at the centre. The poetic place-name of BELOEIL is the leitmotif of the maze's pathways, arranged in the shape of a giant Minoan 'labrys', or double-headed axe. The design also portrays the five-jewelled crown of Prince Antoine de Ligne, a hooded hunting falcon, and a carp fish with which the château's grand canal is abundantly stocked. The route to the goal spells out the anagram BELLE IO, recalling the classical myth of the lovely nymph Io who was pursued by Jupiter. Io changed into a female minotaur, half-woman, half-cow, and escaped his amorous advances by fleeing to Egypt, the land of the pyramids.

Plan of the design of the maze at Château de Beloeil, Belgium.

The maze at Longleat is the largest garden hedge maze in the world. The hairpin turns add to the puzzlement. Bridges provide an extra dimension.

LONGLEAT MAZE

The world's largest hedge maze is at Longleat House in Wiltshire. Lord Weymouth wanted to create a hedge maze on a scale in keeping with this famous Elizabethan house. First opened to the public in 1978, the maze was designed by Greg Bright and although it bears no formal relationship to the house and gardens it includes various innovative puzzle features. Six bridges are used to create a three-dimensional puzzle. Spiral junctions are intended to create confusion by repetition. Elongated fork junctions are cunningly used, since visitors are thought to prefer to 'conserve their momentum' instead of making U-turns. The whirling lines and the lack of any rectangular grid add to the disorientation of this puzzle maze.

HEVER CASTLE MAZE

Henry VIII came to court Anne Boleyn at Hever Castle, the home of the Boleyn family from 1462 until 1538, and it is tempting to imagine him pursuing her along the paths of the maze, although the maze was not created for another four hundred years. This ancient Kentish castle dates back to the thirteenth century, but it was in 1903 that it gained its final historical twist. William Waldorf Astor, the American millionaire, bought Hever Castle and in his scheme of restoration and transformation, added a 'Tudor' village and a unique Italian garden, to accommodate his extensive collection of statuary and antiquities. The yew maze and a set of topiary chessmen were laid out between the two moats to recreate a Tudor atmosphere. The combination of moats, yew hedges, and a classic medieval castle makes Hever Castle one of the most sensational period landscapes of its kind.

Fortunately the vast expanse of yew hedge at Longleat does not need to be clipped by hand. Nevertheless the task still takes several days to complete.

Aerial view of Hever Castle, Kent, showing the magnificent hedge maze and its relationship to the rest of the formal gardens and the castle itself.

SOMERLEYTON MAZE

The Somerleyton maze was laid out in 1846 by William Nesfield. Its charm arises from the generous scale on which it was laid out, and the delightful pavilion at its centre on a large raised mound. The design of the maze is identical to that at Worden Park in Lancashire, since both mazes were built for the same family.

The yew hedges are still the original ones planted in 1846. By the 1970s, they had become excessively thick, and over six feet wide. The bold decision was taken to thin them down. To do this, just one side of the hedge was pruned right back to the stem, and allowed to resprout and strengthen for three years. Only when this had been fully achieved, was the same process applied to the other side of the hedge. After six years, this daring renovation technique was vindicated, by proving entirely successful, and no parts of the hedge were lost. This is a great tribute to the longevity and appropriateness of yew as a superb hedging material for mazes.

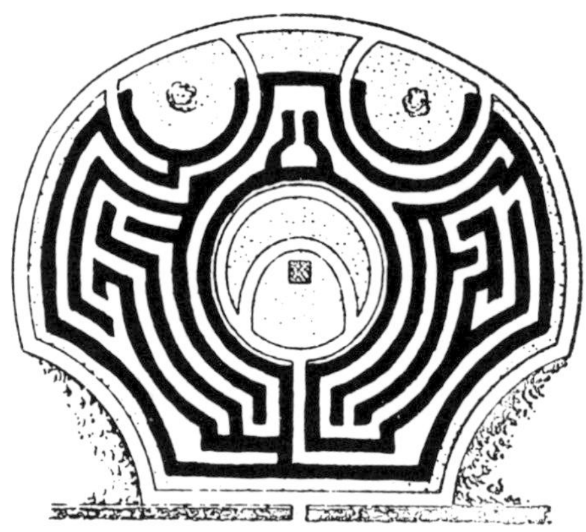

Plan of the maze at Somerleyton.

The raised central pavilion at Somerleyton permits an overview of the maze once the goal has been reached.

'Imprint', a hedge maze design in the shape of a foot in a private garden in Gloucestershire.

'IMPRINT'

The shape of a maze is often suggested by the land, its content by the landowner. Randoll Coate conceived this privately-owned maze whilst in Circeo, Italy, where the proximity of the Cyclopean wall, of the giant sorceress herself, suggested the idea of the footprint of a Colossus – the imprint of man on earth, an imprint such as would be left by a giant as tall as the Eiffel Tower. The patterns of the maze hedges contain the four fundamental symbols of man, the two sexes, the Trinity, the four elements, the five senses, the ten planets, the twelve signs of the zodiac, and so on. For the owner's children, there is a Noah's Ark, and some thirty animals of the English countryside in this Gloucestershire setting. The design for the foot grew until it was too big for its destined field. As a river swirls round one end of it, a dramatic solution had to be found: an island built in the river in the shape of the foremost toe!

NEW HARMONY MAZE

The Harmony Society was a German protestant sect which emigrated to America in 1803 led by George Rapp. They built a vine hedge maze in 1814 at Harmony, Indiana, their second settlement, to symbolize the spirit of their movement, and the difficulty of achieving harmony. The Scottish socialist Robert Owen established a Utopian colony there in 1824, but the maze held no meaning for his followers and it fell into neglect in the 1840s.

In 1939, a new maze of privet was planted near the site of the original maze. There is a rough stone pavilion at its centre containing Harmonist quotations. Rough and crude outside, but elegant and beautiful within, this building is said to reflect the Harmonists' character.

RIGHT AND OPPOSITE *The hedge maze at New Harmony, Indiana, and the design according to which it was planted.*

BELOW *The design for the maze at Leeds Castle is apparently simple. The exit from the maze via an underground grotto is an unexpected surprise.*

LEEDS CASTLE MAZE

Leeds Castle, Kent, described by Lord Conway as 'the loveliest castle in the world', is set on two islands in the middle of a lake. A ninth-century thane named Ledian originally erected a wooden fortress on the site. Queen Eleanor, wife of Edward I, was the first of several Queens of England to live there. In 1974 Lady Baillie, the last private owner, set up a charitable trust to maintain the castle for the nation and for the enjoyment of all, to assist Medicine, and to encourage the Arts.

The formal hedge maze, opened on 25 May 1988 by Princess Alexandra, tempts visitors beyond the Culpeper Gardens and the Aviary. The maze is a topiary castle with castellated yew hedges, an entrance bridge and a central tower. Inside, the maze puzzle is challenging and teasing in several ways. From its central raised goal, the view from its stone parapet rewards the visitor with images of a Queen's crown and a chalice, both laid out in the rows of the hedges.

Looking down, visitors see splashing water and light twenty feet below them. Beneath the stone tower, they discover the entrance to an

underground grotto decorated with thousands of sea shells, with statues in niches, and water cascading over a grotesque face in the manner of the Bomarzo giants in Italy. Still deeper, a ninety foot underground passage beneath the hedges of the maze leads through a dramatic vortex, confronting visitors with a flooded cave, the seat of the nymph of the grotto, before they ascend to the outside world.

THE JUBILEE MAZE

Built by brothers Lindsay and Edward Heyes, the Jubilee Maze is a popular attraction in the Wye Valley in England. The style is that of a Labyrinth of Love, popular between 1560 and 1650, although none now remain. A period atmosphere is created by the brothers dressing in white flannels, blazers and boater hats, and giving a personal greeting to every visitor to the maze. Once inside the maze you are invited to indulge in a gentle game of tag or hide and seek, whilst the brothers may surprise you by appearing on stilts, or riding by on a unicycle. The goal of this fragrant maze of Lawson's cypress hedges is a stone pavilion, floodlit from dusk in August. After solving the maze visitors can enjoy a view from a raised platform, overlooking the maze. There is also an informative Museum of Mazes, and an intriguing puzzle shop.

ABOVE *The spectacular setting of Leeds Castle in Kent makes it the ideal location for a formal hedge maze.*

The Jubilee Maze at Symonds Yat in Hertfordshire is planted in the fast-growing Lawson's cypress.

The maze at Blenheim is the largest symbolic hedge maze in the world. Planted in yew it fits well within the grandeur of Capability Brown's parkland. The tapestry clearly shows all the different elements of the design.

ROSAMUND'S BOWER AND THE MARLBOROUGH MAZE

The Grinling Gibbons carving on the roof of Blenheim Palace provided the inspiration for the maze design.

Woodstock Park, in which Blenheim Palace is situated, contains the site of one of history's most colourful and tragic mazes. The exact site of the fabled Rosamund's Bower is marked by a well and fountain.

'Fair Rosamund', daughter of Walter de Clifford, was mistress to Henry II (1133–1189). Henry built this elaborate maze to conceal Rosamund from his queen, Eleanor of Aquitaine. Rosamund's Bower was probably a most cunning and elaborate architectural maze, with solid walls, stout doors, and other physical defences to provide a haven for their illicit lovemaking. Finally however, in about 1176, Queen Eleanor managed to penetrate the maze, and confronted Rosamund with the choice of a dagger or poisoned chalice – Rosamund chose the poison and died, and it is said that King Henry never smiled again.

The Elizabethan poet Drayton depicted the bower as an arrangement of subterranean vaults, whilst in 1765, Bishop Percy's collection of poetry and English ballads included:

'Most curiously that Bower was built
 Of stone and timber strong.
An hundred and fifty dores
 Did to this Bower belong,
And they so cunningly contriv'd
 With turnings round about
That none but with a clew of thread
 Could enter in or out.'

Woodstock Park was the first enclosed park in England, and Woodstock Palace, long since destroyed, was built by Henry I on the north side of the present lake. Centuries later, a grateful nation built Blenheim Palace within Woodstock Park, and gave it to the First Duke of Marlborough in recognition of his military victories of Blenheim, Ramillies, Oudenard and Malplaquet, in the Wars of the Spanish Succession, 1704–9. The palace was later the birthplace of Winston Churchill, Britain's greatest war leader of the twentieth century.

The inspiration for the Marlborough Maze came from stone sculptures depicting the Panoply of Victory, carved by Grinling Gibbons for the roof of Blenheim Palace. Seen from above, the lines of yew hedges portray pyramids of cannonballs, a cannon firing, and the air filled with banners, flags and the sound of trumpets. The maze has two entrances to left and right, with a central exit. The two wooden bridges create a three-dimensional puzzle, as well as giving tantalising views across parts of the world's largest symbolic hedge maze.

ABOVE *'Oh dear! Oh dear! I shall be too late!' said the White Rabbit who first attracted Alice's attention to the Rabbit-hole.*

OPPOSITE *'The Mock Turtle sang . . . very slowly and sadly', while he danced with the Gryphon.*

FAR RIGHT *Tenniel's Dodo handing Alice the thimble she had just given to him as a prize.*

ALICE-IN-WONDERLAND MAZE

The Alice-in-Wonderland Maze is the centrepiece of Russell Lucas-Rowe's new seven-acre garden at Merritown House in Dorset. Entered under a viewing bridge, this hedge maze contains gigantic shapes within its design. In this topsy-turvy dream world, none of the images are the same way up, but they are all the right way up when seen from the top of the central mound. Rotating clockwise, the principal characters in the story are portrayed in the style of Tenniel's original illustrations – Alice, the Mad Hatter, the White Rabbit, the Cheshire Cat, the Queen of Hearts, the Gryffon, the Mock Turtle and the Dodo. The centre of the maze portrays the White Rabbit's pocket watch, with steps up and down the mound indicating the time at four o'clock, perpetual tea-time. The central octagon is also the body of a giant tea-pot, with the Dormouse sleeping in its handle. Finally, along a short exit, visitors leave the maze just like the ending of Alice's dream, in a flurry of playing cards.

Tapestry showing the Alice-in-Wonderland design for the garden hedge maze at Merritown House in Dorset.

THE ITALIANATE MAZE

The Italianate Maze forms one of a series of period gardens recreated at Capel Manor, and represents the nineteenth century. In England during the 1830s and 1840s, Italianate gardens were all the rage. Several hedge mazes in the Italian style were planted, including one in Bridge End Gardens at Saffron Walden, and others following William Nesfield's designs at Somerleyton Hall, Worden Park, and South Kensington. Although this is not a direct copy of any single maze, the Capel Manor design brings together characteristic elements of the Italianate maze style. These include a neat perimeter with semicircular ends, each semicircle divided into four, a half-span shift in the central parallel section, and four delicate apses within the central goal.

Plan of the Italianate maze at Capel Manor, which is just one element of a large scheme of formal gardens.

The knot garden at Hatfield House. One section of it is laid out in a maze pattern.

The full-size hedge maze at Hatfield planted in yew.

TWO MAZES AT HATFIELD HOUSE

Hatfield House has two fine mazes, although neither is open to the public. The full-height yew hedge maze was planted in 1840 on the bottom terrace of the private gardens below the east front of the house, and is thought to replace an even earlier one. The hedges of the smaller maze are only a few inches high, in the parterre style and can be viewed from above. Planted in *Buxus sempervirens*, it forms a part of Lady Salisbury's design for a Tudor garden in front of the Old Palace at Hatfield. The popular misconception that mazes are often made of box probably arises from the rectangular clipped shapes of a hedge maze, which appear to be box-shaped.

Seaside Holiday Mazes

MAZES CAN BE part of the fun of going away on holiday to the seaside. If there is a maze at a resort, visitors usually expect it to be made of hedges, even though not all hedge materials grow well in the salty sea air. The earlier mazes were usually established within walking distance of the seafront, since holidaymakers generally reached the resort by train or charabanc and then walked everywhere. This explains the location of the hedge mazes at Victoria Park and the Esplanade, both in Scarborough, Blackpool Pleasure Beach, Newquay Zoo, and the maze formerly at Morecambe.

Wider car ownership allows the traditional seaside holiday resort to double as a touring centre for inland day trips. Within a few miles of major resorts are the mazes at the Lappa Valley Railway near Newquay, Blackgang Chine on the Isle of Wight, Bicton Park and the Dart Valley Railway in south Devon, and the Alice-in-Wonderland maze near Bournemouth.

Modern jet travel has now turned entire regions into worldwide vacation destinations. The puzzle maze at Magic Harbor in South Carolina, and the Dolphin Maze at St Petersburg's Poynter Park in Florida are now part of a rapidly growing international trend.

The Dolphins Maze was designed for Poynter Park in downtown St Petersburg, Florida. The idea arose from the 1990 Maze exhibition in Great Explorations Hands-on Museum in St Petersburg. The maze design captures the spirit of Florida, with its vitality and wonderful sealife. These dolphins are portrayed in the style of dolphins painted on ancient Cretan vases, thus making an allegorical allusion to ancient Crete, the home of the most famous labyrinth of all.

The Esplanade Maze is one of two privet mazes planted in Scarborough between 1959 and 1963. The other is in Victoria Park. One of the disadvantages of privet is that it is fast growing and therefore needs clipping several times a year.

ABOVE AND RIGHT *The Bicton maze is in the shape of a giant footprint. The maze paths run between rows of upright wooden posts. If you keep turning consistently left (or right) all round the maze, you will simply come back to the entrance, after going in and out of each of the five toes. A ride on the roundabout in the heel may help solve the puzzle: when it stops, follow the maze path immediately opposite you. The goal is in the ball of the foot.*

DRAGON MAZE

Ancient mythical creatures are often feared within labyrinths, but at Newquay Zoo the mythical beast is the labyrinth itself. One can imagine this menacing creature occupying the nearby St Michael's Mount until the advent of Christianity, when life would have got too hot for dragons. Whatever his misty past, the keepers have now found a safe place for him, and given him a paddock all to himself at the zoo. Since Newquay is in Cornwall, the dragon enjoys the protection of the Duke of Cornwall, the Heir Apparent, and so wears about his neck the heraldic label of three points.

Inside the Dragon Maze. The hedges are of eleagnus, a relatively unusual medium for hedge mazes, but nevertheless creating a good texture.

OPPOSITE *Aerial view of the Dragon Maze at Newquay Zoo in Cornwall.*

Mazes of Brick Paths in Grass

TRADITIONAL TURF MAZES have one fundamental problem – their turf paths simply cannot withstand being walked upon by large numbers of visitors. The Breamore Miz-Maze is a mile from the nearest road, yet has to be closed from time to time, simply for the turf to recover from being worn down to the chalk below.

The innovative solution is to reverse roles, so the turf becomes the barrier, with a firm path to take the weight of visitors. The Saffron Walden turf maze has been restored with a brick path, but due to the narrowness of the paths, only a single row of bricks, laid end to end, was possible. The smallest comfortable width is about a foot wide, so three rows of bricks, thirteen inches wide, is ideal. Alternatively, stone paving can be used. The turf strips need to be wide enough to discourage cheating. Visually, there is a sensational contrast in textures between the living grass, and the mosiac-like nature of the brickwork. Maintenance is simple – mowing straight across like a lawn, and a few hours' edging just twice a year in temperate climates.

Since a much longer path can fit into a small area, and visitors can see and hear each other easily, the experience of solving such mazes is quite different. On the Archbishop's Maze, children usually follow the paths meticulously and it becomes important to them that everyone else does too. A group of children on the maze may suddenly stop playing and call out, if any one of them tries to cheat. Yet their earnest parents often ignore the maze paths, walk determinedly to the centre, briefly inspect the inscriptions, and then look around for the

ABOVE *Edward Hulse boldly made available the site for a maze at his Breamore Countryside Museum in Hampshire, before knowing what the design was to be. Fortunately he was also on the judging panel in the* Sunday Times Magazine*'s 1983 design-a-maze competition. Ian Leitch's winning maze design, of four interlocking five-bar gates, was built full-size, with a topiary yew ewe at its centre.*

At the ancient mizmaze at Breamore in Hampshire the paths are of turf which gets badly worn by its many visitors.

next thing to do. The pressures of their busy and responsible lives are simply too great for them to slow down, even in a country garden. Meanwhile the grandparent generation are truly in their second childhood. I have seen one couple in their eighties, arm-in-arm, leisurely sauntering the entire length of the maze, enjoying every minute of it. They had all the time in the world – and the wit to appreciate it.

THE LAPPA MAZE

The Lappa Maze represents the world's first locomotive, built by the Cornish inventor Richard Trevithick. His historic engine predated the more famous ones built by the Stephensons, such as 'Locomotion' and 'Rocket'.

The brick paths portray Trevithick's 1804 Tramroad Locomotive, with its vast flywheel and interacting pattern of cogs, to a scale of eight times the size of the original engine. The centre of the small driving cog is the goal, reached by following the huge connecting rod from the pistons. On the driving wheels, visitors turn tightly to and fro between the meshing cogs; on the immense flywheel, children can run in imitation of the whirling speed of its circumference.

Hidden within the design are the giant letters 'T' for Trevithick and 'L' for Lappa; the date of Trevithick's Locomotive, 1804, expressed in Roman figures, 'MDCCCIIII'; and 'E.W.R.' for the East Wheal Rose Mine, beside which the maze is sited.

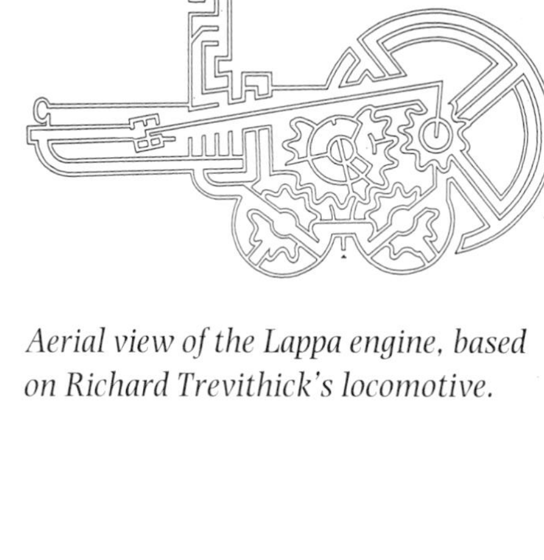

Aerial view of the Lappa engine, based on Richard Trevithick's locomotive.

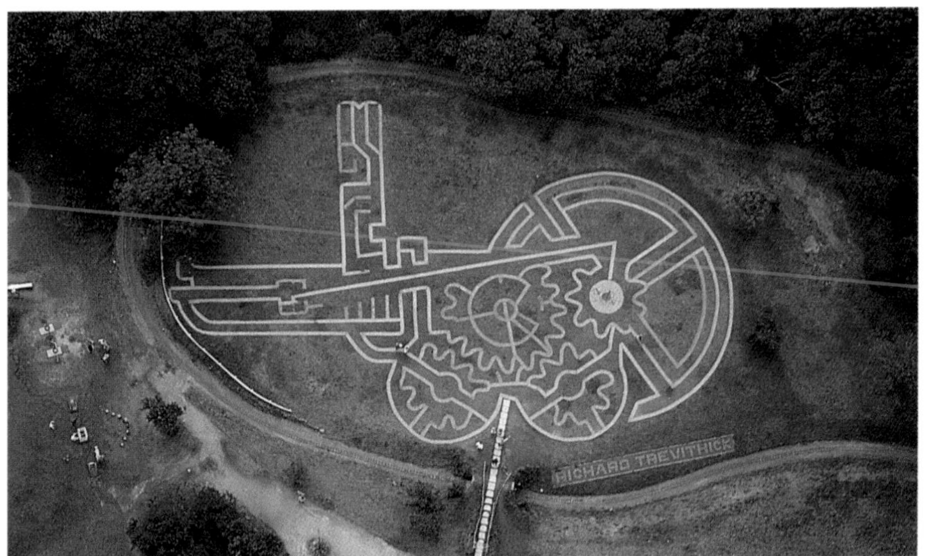

Plan of the Lappa maze in Cornwall.

THE ARCHBISHOP'S MAZE

In his enthronement address when becoming Archbishop of Canterbury (25 March 1980), Robert Runcie spoke of a maze: '*I had a dream of a maze. There were some people very close to the centre, but they could not find a way through. Just outside the maze others were standing. They were further away from the heart of the maze, but they would be there sooner than the party that fretted and fumed inside.*'

The building of a maze in response to this sermon was the inspired idea of Lady Brunner. The maze abounds in Christian symbolism: its cruciform shape, the image of the Crown of Thorns, the seven days of Creation, the nine hours of Agony and the twelve Apostles. At the centre, a simple Roman cross of Bath stone is laid within an elaborate Byzantine cross of blue Westmorland stone. These proclaim the reconciliation between East and West, Catholic and Protestant, Roman and Orthodox – a vital aspect of Robert Runcie's life work.

In one sense, the maze is a puzzle, and there are various junctions with choices to be made. However, by crossing straight over each diamond-shaped thorn, one walks the entire quarter-mile path of the maze. This route represents the Path of Life. At the last turn before reaching the centre, the path goes past the diamond-shaped inscription: 'This maze was dedicated by Robert Runcie, Archbishop of Canterbury, 24th October 1981.' At the centre, an inscribed pillar supports an armillary sundial, which places the visitor exactly in space and time.

The Archbishop's Maze employs brick in its path to prevent the turf from becoming worn out. The design has both a unicursal and a multicursal element. The four faces of the pillar are inscribed with lines from Augustine, Julian of Norwich, Siegfried Sassoon and Robert Gittings.

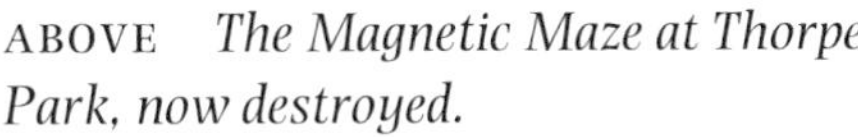

ABOVE *The Magnetic Maze at Thorpe Park, now destroyed.*

BELOW *This artist's impression of the Magnetic Maze design shows the three towers.*

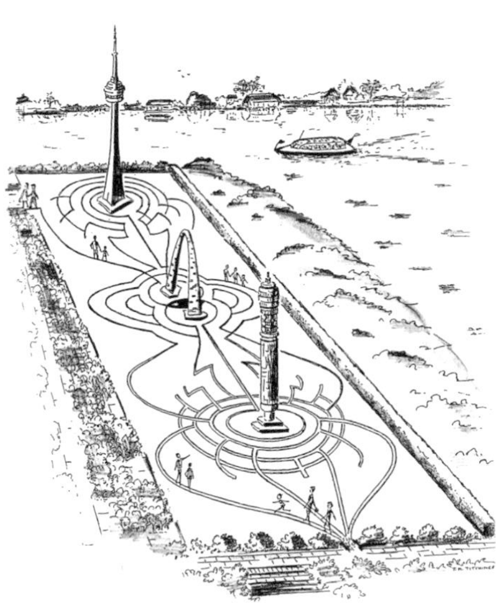

THE MAGNETIC MAZE

The site at Thorpe Park already contained detailed 1:36 scale models of London's Telecom Tower, the Jefferson Memorial Arch in St Louis, USA, and Toronto's Canadian National Tower. The design task was to create a network of maze paths that accurately reflected the existing positions of these models. There is a parallel in science to this situation: whenever magnets are placed on a surface, a magnetic field will develop with no lines of force crossing. The maze was designed by placing magnets on a plan of the positions of the models, and plotting the magnetic field created. This creates a set of swirling paths which never cross.

Two of the towers transmit radio, TV and micro-electronic waves, undetectable by the human senses. Thorpe Park is also strongly based on the theme of water. Concentric rings of maze paths around the models echo both these ideas. These two sets of natural lines were combined to form a spider's web of paths. The flipping from magnetic lines to concentric rings represent the two axes of this strange geometry. The maze design of nearly half a mile of paths began to evolve.

The final twist came with the decision that the maze should have brick paths set in grass. A three-dimensional puzzle maze, paradoxically completely flat, was made by portraying brick 'bridges', as on a map, thus creating a puzzle maze with a magnetic fourth dimension.

Wooden Mazes

COMPARE THE TRANQUIL grace of European garden hedge mazes with the complex against-the-clock puzzle of Japanese wooden mazes. These two maze forms are half a world apart in every sense. With one eye on the clock for an hour or more, runners rush from timeclock to timeclock, to attain instant fame on the display board as the fastest solver of the day. These mazes are immensely popular in Japan, where this competitive and industrious nation flocks in its millions to such attractions.

Different wooden mazes have different objectives. Some provide each visitor with a personal souvenir time card, with the idea being to reach four towers in turn, beneath which is one of four letter stamps which together will spell the word MAZE. The time when each tower is reached is also punched onto the card. The puzzle is fully three-dimensional, with paths going under and over wooden bridges. Sometimes there are also one-way rotating gates, to prevent visitors retracing their way back to previously known positions. The wall panels can be moved and refixed, and the maze design adjusted each day, depending on the expected numbers of visitors. The puzzle is made easier at peak times, to get more visitors through, and harder to solve at quieter times of the week. Perhaps the popularity of different maze types in various countries tells us something about national temperament – compare the single-mindedness and competitiveness of the Japanese approach with the relaxed qualitative emphasis of mazes created by the native tribes of Arizona.

Detail of the labyrinth at Noda City, Japan. Note how the internal walls are taller than the average man to maximize confusion.

Maze at Noda City, Japan.

LEFT OPPOSITE *Complex wooden puzzle maze complete with bridges and a giant red apple at the centre; Japan.*

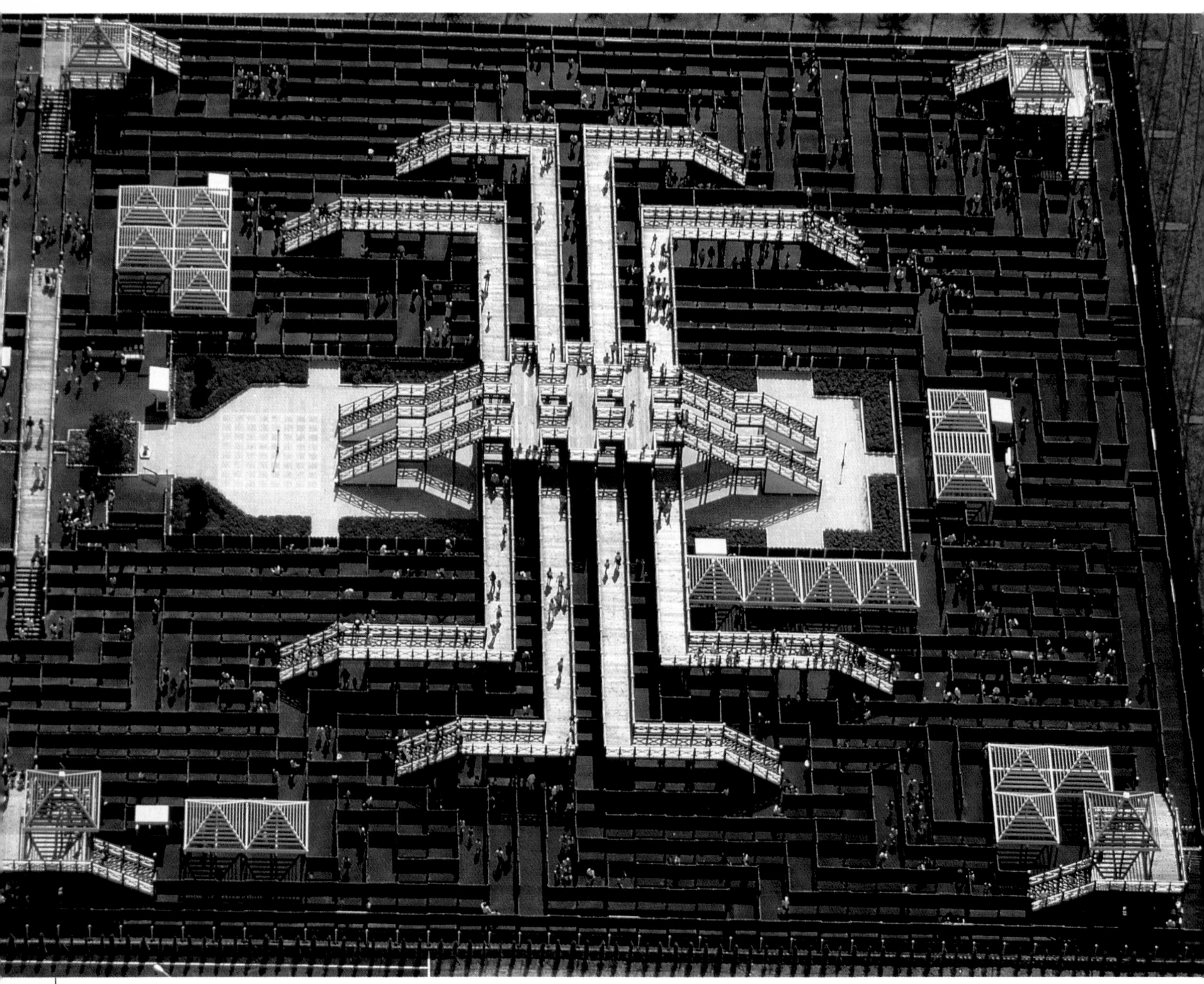

Maze at Funabushi, Japan.

The development of modern wooden mazes was pioneered by Stuart Landsborough, an Englishman who settled in Wanaka, New Zealand, and built a maze with wooden bridges, and a puzzle shop. He has since designed and built many wooden mazes, mostly in Japan, with others in New Zealand and Australia. At their peak of popularity in 1987, Japan had over two hundred wooden mazes, each using wooden panels and overhead bridges to pack in the maximum number of alleyways, in the country with the world's highest land values. Over sixty mazes have since been demolished, as even more profitable uses are found for the land areas they occupy.

ABOVE *Fiendish puzzle maze at Yokohama, Japan.*

Maze within a maze at Bullsbrook, near Perth, Western Australia.

Courtyard Mazes

THE MOST CONCISE outdoor maze settings are intimate courtyards, whether enclosed by stone castles, monastic cloisters, Tudor houses or university quadrangles. Overlooked on all sides at different heights by dozens of windows, a courtyard maze design can revel in exquisite paved detail made with fine materials. The advantages of a pavement maze over low planted parterres or knots are its durability, ease of maintenance, and the fact that it can be walked upon, thus enriching the community life of the courtyard and surrounding buildings.

At Madresfield Court near Malvern, the Beauchamp family has a courtyard pavement maze, which complements the fine hedge maze in their grounds. These two private mazes were created in the late nineteenth century.

The Tudor courtyards of Temple Newsam House near Leeds and Kentwell Hall in Suffolk both have brick pavement mazes. At Kentwell, the paving bricks create vigorous patterns on a scale that can be walked upon. On a reinforced concrete foundation, the paviors are laid on a bed of mortar, with mortar grouting. This is quite different from other methods of brick paving, and demands great bricklaying skill to achieve a sensational result. Different brick colours are carefully selected and matched, since the overall weight of colour is also important.

Temple Newsam House near Leeds derives its name from the Knights Templar, who are thought to have had a significant role in the design of medieval Christian pavement mazes. The main courtyard of Temple Newsam House is one of the largest Tudor courtyards in England. Early engravings of the courtyard show a labyrinthine pattern laid out diagonally. The present maze was built in 1978 to recapture the spirit of its original appearance. Its brick paths between gravel provide two contrasting textures.

Aerial view of the Tudor Rose pavement maze at Kentwell Hall, Suffolk.

THE TUDOR ROSE MAZE

The Tudor Rose Maze fills the main courtyard of moated Kentwell Hall near Long Melford in Suffolk. Using twenty-seven thousand red and white paving bricks, it is thought to be the world's largest brick pavement maze. Set in the design are fifteen diamonds of etched brick, decorated with symbols representing the Tudors.

The maze design simultaneously offers a five-fold unicursal labyrinth, a maze puzzle, and at the centre a giant chess board. The five separate progressions through the maze, from the five outer thorns to the centre, echo the internal rotational symmetry hidden within Classical and medieval Christian labyrinths. Alternatively, the rose becomes a three-dimensional puzzle maze, by observing the junctions and flyovers indicated by the brick paths.

This unique combination of entertainments in the design of the Tudor Rose was built to celebrate five hundred years since the start of the Tudor dynasty in 1485, and won the British Tourist Authority's 'Heritage in the Making' Award.

Mazes in the City

IN CITY CENTRES land and space are at a premium. Equally, greater resources are available to create a fine and stimulating environment. This opens the way to using a wider range of materials in maze construction, including high quality paving, mosaic, sculpture, fountains and brickwork.

Suitable locations for a city centre maze include Georgian squares, modern city plazas, covered shopping malls and pedestrianised streets. The latter are extended linear areas sometimes only a dozen paces across. With the opportunity to look down from surrounding buildings, these level surfaces provide areas for innovative design, and pavement mazes stimulate street activity.

The city centre public park has many roles to play. It is an attractive contrast to pavements and streets, and provides a refreshing thoroughfare to walk through. Office workers come to eat their packed lunches, tourists to relax or study their maps, courting couples to meet, and theatregoers to take the air. Suburban public parks, on the other hand, are a local community resource, with families coming to play, seeing them as an extension to their own private gardens.

Warren Street underground station in central London offers an irresistible visual pun on the word warren. This striking ceramic black and red tile maze is used as a wall motif up and down the platforms. At ground level, a few hundred yards away, the Warren Street children's playground has a brick pavement maze, loosely based on the medieval Christian maze design.

ABOVE *Tapestry of the Unicorn design created to pair with the Lion in Worksop town centre pedestrian precinct.*

LEFT *The Lion Rampant pavement maze in Worksop town centre.*

THE LION AND UNICORN MAZES

The Lion Rampant and Unicorn Rampant brick pavement mazes are keynote features at each end of the Worksop Town Centre pedestrian area. A strong heraldic theme was chosen for the whole scheme, based on the five Dukeries of Nottinghamshire. Lions appear in the heraldic devices of the Dukes of Norfolk and Kingston, and the Lion and Unicorn are paired in the Royal Family's Coat of Arms.

Laid in various colours of paving brick, they are both exciting designs and also puzzling mazes to solve. Visitors enter at the foot, and the goal is the top of the creature's head. The maze paths, partly within the body and partly outside, run between the darker lines of the design.

The maze in the Beazer Gardens in Bath.

The Gorgon's Head at the centre of the Bath Festival Maze. Gold tesserae are used to indicate the path to the goal in the manner of Ariadne's thread.

THE BATH FESTIVAL MAZE

'The Maze' was chosen as the theme for the 1984 Bath Festival, as expressed in music, opera, painting, sculpture, literature and film. It included a major exhibition of the work of the English sculptor and painter Michael Ayrton.

It was decided to build a full-size permanent maze in the heart of the City of Bath, in the Beazer Gardens on the River Avon, immediately below Pulteney Bridge. Set in grass, the Bath stone paths describe an elegant ellipse, recalling the Georgian fanlights above the doors of Bath, the Brunel railway arches and the shape of the nearby Pulteney weir. Paradoxically the path to the goal is always shortened by taking turnings away from the centre. The maze can also be solved by going straight over each junction, when every path in the maze is walked once and once only.

At the centre is a mosaic, fifteen feet in diameter, containing an enlarged representation of the famous Gorgon's Head. The central mosaic, otherwise known as the Sun god Sul, cult figurehead from the Temple of Sulis Minerva in Bath, is surrounded by six apses which celebrate the four seasons and Bath's Celtic and Roman past. The six apses represent: Proserpina, Goddess of Spring, scattering flowers before the temple of Sulis Minerva. She evokes Bath, the City of Flowers; dolphins, beloved Sea Creatures of the Ancients, a favourite adornment of Roman baths; the Swine of Bladud, legendary founder of Bath, coursing through the Autumn forest into the magic mire, which cured the herdsman's leprosy and restored him to kingship; Orpheus, son of Apollo, who charmed the beasts of creation with his music, personifying Bath's Summer Festival of the Arts; the Winged Horse, Pegasus, kicking Mount Helicon and releasing the fountains of poetry, thus symbolizing both the city of the arts and the city as a watering place; surprised in the winter darkness of the labyrinth, the Minotaur awaiting his executioner; Theseus is heralded by the flames of seasonal death.

The mosaic is of Italian marble, and is made up of over seventy-two thousand mosaic pieces in fifteen different colours. The Gorgon's Head and the six surrounding apses comprise seven gaze-mazes. The central gaze-maze, containing the Gorgon, uses gold Venetian glass to recreate the meandering course of Ariadne's golden thread. Perceptive visitors will detect an oblique allusion to the maze in Chartres Cathedral, through the use of a circular central area ringed by six semicircular apses.

The Dolphin gaze-maze, part of the Bath Festival Maze.

Aerial view of the maze in Bath which is located next to the river in the Beazer Gardens near the famous Pulteney Bridge.

CATHAY PACIFIC
SunLife of Canada

Water Mazes

WATER CREATES AN irresistible attraction within the landscape. A narrow stream or rill, running in a prepared stone or brick channel, has long been a favourite landscape feature. The Bristol Water Maze has eleven rings of tightly coiled brick channels for its water to run in. At Rousham in Oxfordshire in 1737, William Kent created his celebrated rill, running and curving the length of a woodland path in a shallow stone channel. The gardens of Mughal India displayed various imaginative water effects of an essentially labyrinthine nature. In Japan, the *Haiku* is a formal three-line poem with precisely seventeen syllables; a pleasant garden diversion was to compose aloud a *Haiku* in the time one's wine glass took to float through a labyrinthine water channel in the floor of a pavilion. A well-composed *Haiku* typically has a wry twist in its tail.

A larger water surface is visually fascinating, constantly changing as the breeze plays upon it, as well as reflecting the images of reeds, vertical elements and people beyond. An open area of water can be used in a maze as the barrier between raised brick or stone pathways, or between islands joined by footbridges. When cascading over waterfalls or thrusting upwards as fountains, the compelling movement of water is intensified by the refreshing negative ions that such water releases into the air. Cascading water makes a sensational feature within a maze, as has been achieved within the grotto of the Leeds Castle maze. Thirty-nine sets of fountains were used as features within the allegorical labyrinth at Versailles.

THE BRISTOL WATER MAZE

The course of the Bristol Water Maze in Victoria Park is not a path but a brick channel. Water wells up at the centre, and flows along every part of its eleven rings. A twig or leaf can be slowly floated the entire length, providing ample time for contemplation. Alternatively, the visitor can follow the maze barefoot or in rubber boots. The maze design was copied from the medieval Christian design of the roof-boss maze in St Mary Redcliffe Church. The connection is emphasized by one axis of the maze pointing towards the spire of the church, on the horizon a mile away.

The fifteenth-century wooden roof boss in the north transept of St Mary Redcliffe church, Bristol.

The Bristol Water Maze. The spire of St Mary Redcliffe church can be seen on the horizon.

The Yellow Submarine, the subject of one of the Beatles' most famous songs, was chosen as the goal of the Beatles' Maze. Inside it contained some genuine submarine equipment and twin spiral staircases led up and down the conning tower to give an overview of the maze.

THE BEATLES' MAZE

A celebration of the Beatles' musical achievement seemed fitting and relevant for Liverpool's International Garden Festival in 1984. The Yellow Submarine, one of their most fantastic musical images, was chosen as the centrepiece of an aquatic maze.

The shape of the pool was that of the Beatles' Apple. The brick pathway over the water and among waterlilies delineated the shape of the listening ears of the world. The maze started with four rows of bricks, each representing a Beatle. Passing a statue of John Lennon, the path was reduced to three rows of bricks as a memorial to Lennon's untimely death. The course of the maze stopped tantalisingly short of the submarine and continued as stepping stones representing notes of music before resuming as a brick pathway to the entrance of the submarine.

This eighteen ton, fifty-one foot long creation of the Beatles' unforgettable fantasy was built by some eighty Youth Training Scheme trainees in the Cammell Laird shipyard at Birkenhead. It proved one of the most popular attractions, and was visited by a million people during the six months of the Festival. Opened by HM the Queen, the maze was awarded two gold medals for Design Excellence and the Best Liverpool Theme Garden, and the Yellow Submarine won one of the ten premier prizes, for the most Innovative Garden Structure of the festival.

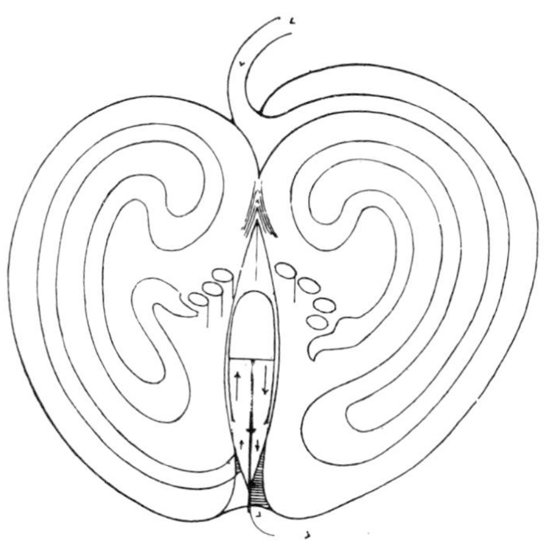

Plan showing the apple shape of the Beatles' Maze.

Artist's impression of the Beatles' Maze which was created for the International Garden Festival in Liverpool in 1987.

The brightly coloured stained glass maze window in the shopping mall at Irvine town centre in Scotland. There is also a small maze in relief on the wall opposite.

Stained Glass Window Mazes

ONE FASCINATION OF stained glass is its rich translucence of colour, which changes with the quality of light at different times of day. Labyrinths have had close associations with stained glass windows ever since the construction of Chartres Cathedral, where the magnificent western rose window is precisely related to the pavement maze.

Any maze portrayed in stained glass is intended to be viewed from a distance, rather than traced with the finger. Inspired by its ancient village turf maze, the parish church at Alkborough has a small maze in the Victorian stained glass window above the main altar. The shopping mall at Irvine town centre in Scotland has a brightly coloured stained glass maze window. Most recently, my own family has included a maze within a stained glass window, in the hall of the Worshipful Society of Apothecaries.

APOTHECARIES' MAZE WINDOW, APOTHECARIES' HALL

The City of London has a maze displayed within a stained glass window in Apothecaries' Hall in Blackfriars, portraying the armorial 'achievement' of a recent Master Apothecary. Does this maze design date back centuries? Not a bit! Both my father and grandfather have been Masters of the Worshipful Society of Apothecaries of London – the City livery company that represents doctors. In 1984 the opportunity arose to apply for a Grant of Arms for my father and the Fisher family in general. So we all went off to the College of Arms, met York Herald, and together discussed what it should contain.

The resulting 'achievement' contains the magic, mystery and family in-jokes that heraldry is so good at portraying. The crest is a magic toad (based on father's nickname Bufo or Bouf) 'about to leap', because he is always about to do something. The fleam, a traditional medical instrument for opening veins, indicates that it's a medical toad. The overall colour scheme of blue and gold recalls the arms claimed by the Mortimer side of the family (Mort Mer – Dead Sea – sand and sky). The serpent of medicine coming out of a meadow or mead represents my great-grandmother Mead who qualified in medicine in 1886. The White Rose recalls our Haythornthwaite forebears who came from Yorkshire, and also refers to my grandfather Reginald Fisher who, like Edmund de Langley, first Duke of York and son of Edward III, was born, died and buried in King's Langley. The maze reflects my own vocation of maze designer, and that repeated decision-making is a characteristic aspect of medical practice. The motto *Primo Perfectus* is the closest Latin

The stained glass window in Apothecaries Hall showing the Fisher coat of arms, complete with maze.

translation of 'Get it Right First Time'. We felt this was a suitably modern motto to aspire to, in a world where technology frees us to do things once and once only, so it must be Right First Time – and it is also a good motto for a maze designer, who never creates the same design twice.

The Riddle of the Maze

The labyrinth idea has proved pervasive and irrepressible. The undoubted visual appeal and the physical experience of walking within the maze are not in themselves sufficient to explain this. The secret of its enduring fascination lies much deeper.

PREVIOUS PAGE *The original stone labyrinth on St Agnes, Scilly Isles. It was rebuilt in 1988.*

THE NUMBER OF mazes open to the public worldwide almost doubled in the 1980s. This renaissance of interest in mazes can be illustrated by the numbers of new mazes built, older ones restored, and by their remarkable diversity and creativity. One aspect of the riddle of the maze is to explain this dramatic reawakening.

In our 'designer' age, there is an underlying truth that precision marketing, meticulous research, effective design and excellent quality are needed to make things happen. One cultural trend has been towards greater formality in all aspects of art and design. Increasing leisure has stimulated a reawakened appreciation of fine gardens and open spaces, and of mazes with their sculptural and almost architectural qualities.

The pace of maze innovation has never been greater with more innovative developments in maze design in one decade than in the previous hundred.

Mazes have proved ideal for today's mass tourism, recreation and family leisure. In Japan, one of the world's most overcrowded countries, more than two hundred mazes were built within five years.

Inner city areas have a special and intensive role, where cars can be banished, and life on foot can take on a new lease of life. As an artefact on a human scale, a maze establishes an oasis of calm and an environment of beauty, where people of all ages can mingle and play, or just stay around and watch.

The present age of information has fuelled mankind's curiosity in all aspects of endeavour, with more historical research being conducted than in any previous generation. Technology provides new research methods — for

When creating a turf garden for the 1990 National Garden Festival at Gateshead, thoughts turned to English village greens, and their distinctive turf mazes. Like ancient turf mazes, the Rolawn turf maze uses the raised grass strip as the path, with the gulley providing the barrier. This turf maze with its five axes contains internal rotational symmetry, which has been a hallmark of such mazes for thousands of years. The five stone balls provide an effective vertical element to the design.

Aerial view of the ancient turf maze at Saffron Walden, Essex, which follows the medieval Christian design.

example a new technique for analysing lichens offers a possible way to date stone labyrinths in Scandinavia. Meticulous field surveys are saving valuable information, before wanton destruction randomly strikes. Aerial photography brings the beauty of remote labyrinths to a wider audience, thus strengthening public resolve to preserve them. Historical interest is stimulating the restoration of mazes – whether the tracing and surveying of ancient labyrinth sites; the protection and repair of surviving turf mazes such as at Breamore and Saffron Walden; or the research and restoration of early hedge mazes such as at Bridge End Gardens, Rhinefield House and Castle Bromwich Hall Gardens.

THE RESTORED HEDGE MAZE IN BRIDGE END GARDENS, SAFFRON WALDEN

Bridge End Gardens in Saffron Walden were laid out from the late eighteenth century to the middle of the nineteenth century. The maze was planted in 1839, with a pavilion, statues, seating and a viewing

RIGHT OPPOSITE *The labyrinth motif appears five times in the Watts Chapel at Compton in Surrey; one is on the altar, and there are four carved labyrinths supported by angels outside the church.*

platform. It remained in active use until the Second World War, after which it became neglected and overgrown. In 1984, Tony Collins and John Bosworth planned to clear the site and replant the maze. Before doing so, they carried out an archaeological investigation which produced fascinating results. A large quantity of oyster shells and the remains of Victorian wine bottles proved that the maze had been well enjoyed over the years.

Tree ring analysis of surviving yews revealed 148 rings; their respective thicknesses indicate different growing conditions. Four phases were evident: first, the young yews were planted in nursery conditions in 1835–6, and grew rapidly; second, when three to four years old, they were transplanted to form the maze, and for twelve years they grew very rapidly in both height and width; third, by 1852 the yews were being regularly trimmed, and growth was suppressed by regular trimming for ninety-seven years; fourth, the yews were left unclipped, and they bolted vigorously upwards for thirty-five years.

Markings on the reverse of the maze pavilion's geometric floor tiles indicated a date of 1841–6, the period when the patent of Richard Prosser's tile process was held by Minton and Co. This is consistent with an 1838–9 planting, as a pavilion would not normally be built until the maze had begun to mature.

Its Italianate design raises the question of whether William Andrews Nesfield may have been involved in its design, despite a lack of documentary evidence supporting this theory. In the 1830s and 1840s, Nesfield was a leading exponent of the Italianate gardening style and, in 1851, as part of the Great Exhibition, he designed an Italianate maze in London with similar design features – semi-circular single and double apses, large semi-circles, and statuary partially hidden within recesses. In his diary in 1837, the owner of Bridge End, Francis Gibson, recorded for a trip to London 'views of gardens, Hampton Court its labyrinth', and this visit may have sparked off the idea of creating a hedge maze. Gibson and Nesfield were fellow members of the Royal Botanic Society, so Nesfield's influence is at least possible.

Plan of the recently restored hedge maze at Bridge End Gardens in Saffron Walden, Essex. It was originally planted in 1839 to an Italianate design and only fell into neglect during the Second World War.

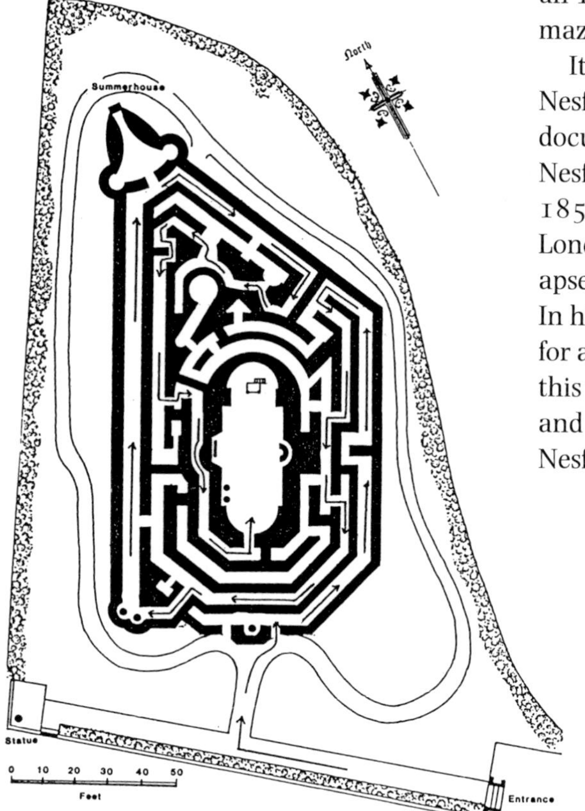

OPPOSITE *The church at Itchen Stoke has a pavement maze fifteen feet in diameter beneath the altar, in russet brown and dark green tiles.*

Increasing awareness of the world's fragile ecological balance is also stimulating a re-evaluation of the spiritual challenges that face mankind. Here again the ubiquitous maze flourishes, whether maintaining a link with the mysterious landscape of the past, or providing a continuing source of inspiration for the modern Christian church. New labyrinths are being created in traditional ways for active, processional and ritual use.

All these factors help explain why today's fascination with mazes has never been greater. But they still do not penetrate the deeper riddle of why the labyrinth has excited such strong interest down the ages, for over four millennia.

The concentric rings of a labyrinth attract attention like a magnet. A maze motif on a page of print instantly draws the human eye, like the slightest movement catching the eye of a hunting leopard. Yet no mere pattern can command such vigorous pervasiveness. Unlike the natural beauty of ribbed sand on a beach, or concentric tree-rings, mazes are man-made, designed for a purpose. That purpose is to be solved. Yet on its own, the physical sensation of walking or running through a maze or labyrinth does not explain their longevity.

Mathematically, the maze is a paradox. Seemingly symmetrical, true symmetry is the one form it can never take, since it must contain an entrance and have an exit to its goal. Puzzle mazes can appear a tough mathematical challenge, yet can yield to intuitive perceptual skills. A maze must have a solution that can be demonstrated; an unsolvable maze would be both invalid and not a maze. Certainly the late twentieth century has shown new ways to play with a maze, from computer maze games to full-size racing mazes in Japan.

The answer seems to lie in the overwhelming human appeal of the maze. Myths and legends ooze from every pore. Stories and anecdotes latch themselves like muscle tissue to the skeletal bones of stone, turf and hedge, bringing this art-form to life as a vibrant part of mankind's culture.

Whether the story is the vigorous explanation of Iitoi disappearing into the labyrinthine mountains, or the words of an archbishop's sermon expressed allegorically in the landscape, the maze has proved a powerful prompt in sustaining an oral tradition on fundamental issues of life and love, security and prosperity, birth and death, earliest origins and life hereafter.

The physical structure of the maze offers a superb framework for a distinctive art-form – part symbolic, part tortuous, part rewarding. By implanting deeper significance within this art-form, mankind has ensured the greater endurance both of the ideas contained within, and of the physical labyrinths themselves.

Like any other art form, the maze has its strengths and its limitations. Stone sculpture has to obey the laws of gravity, and the mechanical weaknesses of slenderness. Similarly, a maze must provide a uniform width of passageway throughout – if paths dilate and contract in width, the feel of the maze pathways begins to be lost. Barriers usually have uniform width, for maximum compression of the design within a given area; moreover, excessively thick hedges tend to grow weak in the middle.

Within its set of design rules, the maze is a liberating art-form. Three waving lines can denote the mane of a unicorn, one intermittent curve a flowing banner of war. The austerity of colour makes any highlight stand out boldly. Its sculptural precision, whether executed as a pavement or created in clipped hedges, gives it an architectural quality, yet on a scale that would be unthinkable as a building. The subtle effect of colour in brick pavement mazes is striking. Maze design shares with heraldry the ability to portray magic, mystery and family traditions.

The maze provides a framework to which symbolism can adhere and grow, until it is not clear whether the skeleton supports the muscles, or the muscles drive the frame. Both elements become indistinguishably essential to the substance of the maze. Indeed, when a maze only aims to be a puzzle, the symbolic aspect and much of its fascination is lost.

Once considered from this perspective, evidence cascades in to reinforce this view. Indeed, it has proved impossible to explain the history and origins of mazes and labyrinths without considering their social, cultural and mythological significance. From the Greek myth of Theseus and the Minotaur and the Arizonan legend of Iitoi, to the virgin dances of Finland and Sweden, the abundant cultural tradition sometimes exceeds the physical manifestation – a remarkable reverse from so many enigmatic archaeological ruins which challenge us to conceive any explanation at all.

Many other labyrinth stories and traditions abound. In Afghanistan, the story of Shamaili's house involves a house with a secret entrance, represented by a labyrinth drawing, which only Princess Shamaili knew how to enter. Her father King Khunkhar 'the bloodthirsty' promised her to the first suitor who could find her, but the penalty for failure was death by hanging. Jallad Khan was the youngest of seven sons of King Namazlum; the other six had all failed and died. Jallad Khan hid himself in a hollow sculpture, which was brought before King Khunkhar, whereupon the sculpture came to life and began to dance. The curious princess took the sculpture to her room. At midnight, Jallad Khan slipped out of the sculpture and exchanged rings with the sleeping princess. The next night the princess spoke to the sculpture, and said 'Come out whoever you are and be my husband'. He came out and spent the next ten nights with her. Then Jallad Khan asked King Khunkhar for permission to marry Shamaili, and she helped him find his way to her house, thus fulfilling the condition of marriage and winning her hand. Jallad Khan finally got his own kingdom, and avenged his dead brothers by putting out the eyes of King Khunkhar.

The Swedish story of Grimborg's bride was enacted in labyrinths created on ice, with paths wide enough for skating. A girl stood at the centre, guarded by a young man, and everyone sang 'the song of Grimborg' as a second man tried to get past the guard to the girl. The song tells how Grimborg forced his way through 'fences of iron and steel' to be with the beautiful daughter of a king. The king attacked, but Grimborg killed twelve thousand of the king's men and escaped with his bride to his mother's house. Surrounded, Grimborg killed another twelve thousand men and then rode alone to the king's house, fought once more, and was rewarded when the king finally allowed him to marry the princess.

The Hopi tribal tradition of northern Arizona has two forms of labyrinth symbol. One is the familiar Classical labyrinth symbolizing the Sun Father, the giver of life; the other is known as Tapu'at (Mother and Child), and which by a very slight reconnection of lines, has one labyrinth inside another. This Mother Earth symbol depicts the unborn child within the womb, and also the newborn baby cradled in its mother's arms.

In Scandinavia, stone labyrinths on the shores of the Baltic were believed to

The two forms of labyrinth used by the Hopi tribe in Northern Arizona. The one BELOW *symbolizes the Mother Earth, enclosing her child, either in the womb or in her arms, as demonstrated by the shading of the two separate labyrinth paths.*

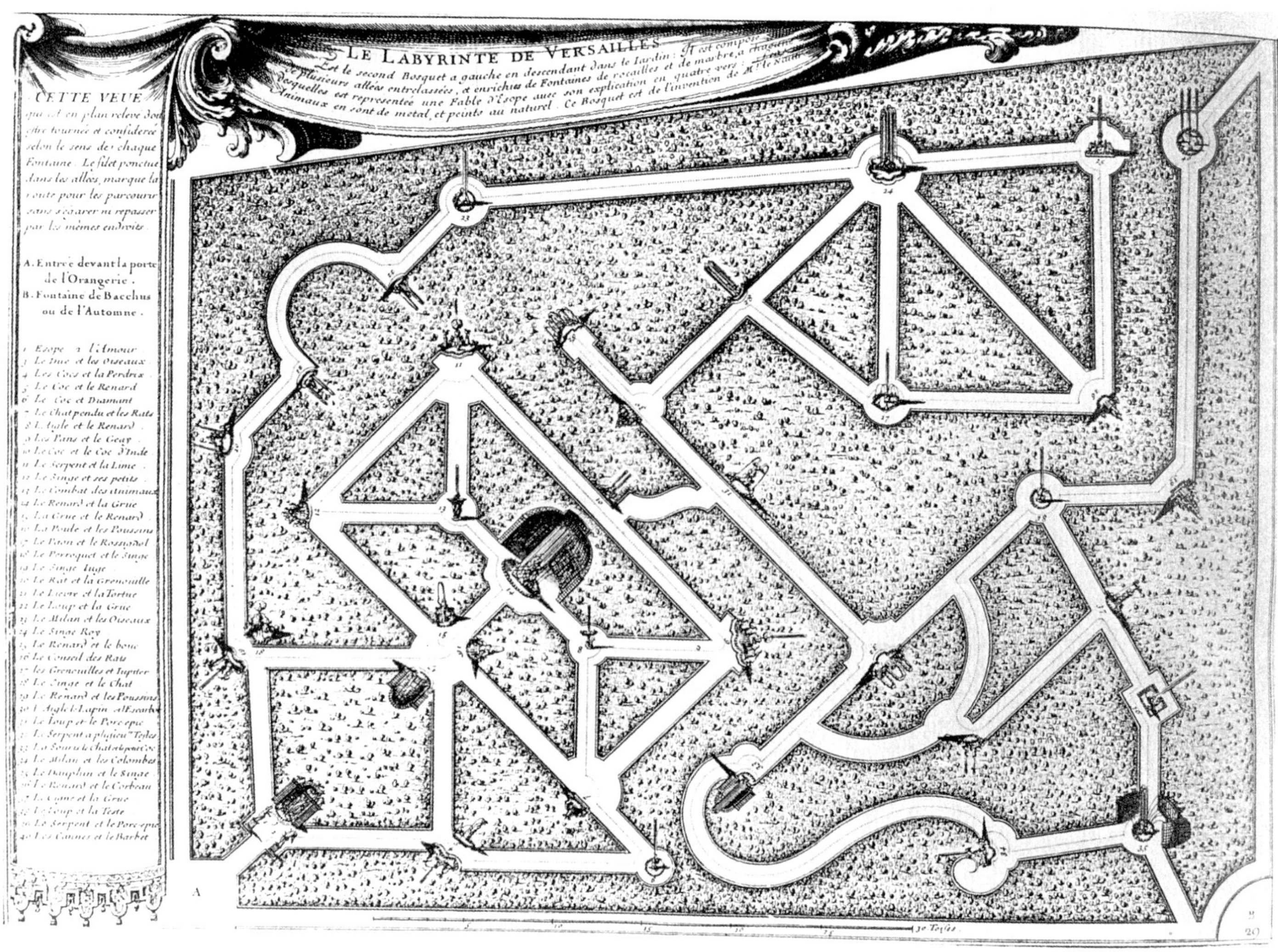

have magic powers over life at sea. Fishermen walked through them in procession before setting off on fishing expeditions, in the hope of controlling the weather, obtaining a good catch, and ensuring a safe return. They would build a stone labyrinth if the weather was too rough to venture forth, in the hope of capturing and containing the force of the storm within the coils of the labyrinth. Certainly it was a diverting way to pass the time, when trapped by bad weather on an offshore island. Fishermen believed that little people (*smagubbar*) could bring bad luck. These 'bad luck people' would try to follow them everywhere. The way to prevent them joining a fishing trip was to walk to the centre of a labyrinth, then run very fast out to the boat and put to sea, leaving the little people behind still stuck in the labyrinth. This has parallels with other traditions, where it is believed that evil spirits cannot turn corners

Plan of the Garden maze at Versailles, based on Aesop's Fables, which was solved by passing each marble statue only once. The dotted line shows how this could be achieved.

easily or at all. For land-based occupations, the magic properties of labyrinths were believed to provide protection against wolves and evil gnomes, and to help with the migration of reindeer.

The place names of ancient stone and turf labyrinths provide further insight. Julian's Bower is often found, with corruptions such as Gillian's Bore, Geylan Bower and St Julians, hinting at the name Gillian as a universal metaphor for girl, as in Jack and Jill. Wherever this commonplace girl's name is found, one may expect the female figure to be found within the labyrinth and honoured for her beauty and fertility. Traditions of courtship, pairing and future fertility follow on from this idea.

In many ways, the labyrinth is a celebration of youth and adolescence. It is an intriguing place for children to play, and young people can race its paths at great speed. The apprentice guilds, such as the shoemakers, used them as a focal point for their maytime revelries. Down the ages, the labyrinth has simply been great fun. It is a place to run, to race, to chase someone else, and to try to catch them. Running in a compact space, onlookers round the edge can share the excitement. On the turf maze at Saffron Walden, early records describe wagers in gallons of beer on the outcome of such races.

Processional labyrinth designs allowed the whole community to join in, without congestion at the centre. The design of stone and turf labyrinths in Sweden, Germany and Poland clearly indicate this processional purpose. The Wyck Rissington maze had a processional path, passing each of the fifteen Mysteries of the Gospels in the correct order; as members of the congregation approached each sign, they could read and contemplate what it meant at that point in the sequence, and thus progress through the maze became a memorable experience. Canon Cheales described this path as the Christian Path of Life.

In Renaissance Europe, the labyrinth proved a perfect vehicle for allegory. The allegorical labyrinth at Versailles portrayed Aesop's Fables, with just one correct route through the labyrinth that passed each fable just once and once only – and in the correct order. Each fable was portrayed by a fountain sculpture, with jets of water representing speech, issuing from the mouth of each creature who spoke in the fable.

One pioneer of the modern art of the maze was Michael Ayrton. In the 1950s, this English sculptor began to identify himself with the myth of the Minotaur and the Labyrinth, and to see it as a symbol of the human condition. Ayrton's first sight of the Acropolis at Cumae, on 11 May 1956, was a profoundly formative experience. It was the place where Daedalus landed after his winged escape from Crete. Ayrton's work took on a bold direction as he explored the depths of the Minoan myth. Even its technology challenged him, and he repeated Daedalus' achievement of casting a golden honeycomb using the wax of a bee, the oldest and purest form of the lost-wax process.

The marble fountain in the Versailles maze representing the fable of the Hare and the Tortoise.

OPPOSITE *Aerial view of the Arkville Maze, New York State, designed by Michael Ayrton.*

Two of Ayrton's finest bronzes, that of the Minotaur and of Daedalus and Icarus are the twin centrepieces of his greatest artefact. Like Daedalus, he finally designed a labyrinth of legendary proportions, with walls of stone and brick ten feet high. One of the most ambitious maze of modern times, this labyrinth was built in 1969 at Arkville, New York State, on the estate of banker Armand Erpf. Ayrton's maze has two central goals, one containing a huge bronze sculpture of the Minotaur, and the other a sculpture of winged Icarus leaping from his father's shoulders to fly upwards.

In our own design work, symbolism is a key ingredient. Many earlier forms of garden design have contained allegorical significance, but the particular nature of the maze allows the expression of symbolism on a grand scale – sometimes extending hundreds of feet across the landscape. The Archbishop's Maze is possibly the epitome of this approach, creating a contemplative atmosphere within its setting. In its own quite different way, the Beatles' Maze at Liverpool's International Garden Festival was fantastically appropriate, capturing the imagination of the people of Liverpool, and implanting the catchy music and words of the song 'Yellow Submarine' into the minds of every visitor. The Alice-in-Wonderland maze near Bournemouth takes a well-known nursery tale, with its familiar illustrations by Tenniel, in order to create a fantasy garden complete with yew topiary and a croquet lawn.

The Minotaur is one of a pair of bronze sculptures occupying the twin goals of the Arkville maze. The picture shows how the walls increase in height as the centre is reached, creating a greater sense of confusion.

'CREATION'

Randoll Coate's design for the Varmlands maze was inspired by the words of the great Swedish botanist Linnaeus, *Omne vivum ex ovo*. Planted in the shape of a falcon's egg, it plays a pun on the family name of Falkenberg.

The maze portrays two different stories. Firstly, telling the story of the Garden of Eden, the lines of the hedges depict the Tree of Knowledge, flanked by Adam and Eve plucking the forbidden fruit. Hidden in the maze design are twenty-two beasts of the Garden of Eden. Visiting 'Adams' and 'Eves' have their separate entrances and, when inside, can only meet in Adam's rib. By unlocking a series of gates, they can find their way to final paradise, the Sun – the yolk of the falcon's egg. The maze, fifty-five by forty-four yards, is entirely measured in multiples of eleven, the cyclic number of the sun.

The second story shown in the rows of hedges is the classical Greek myth of the Labyrinth. As if cut in half by Theseus, the design shows just one half of the Minotaur's head. On the left, Ariadne unravels her golden thread around the top of the design. On the right Icarus, with the wax of his wings melting in the heat of the sun, plummets into the sea.

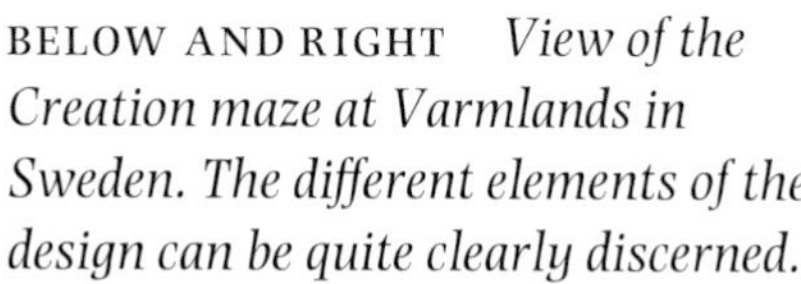

BELOW AND RIGHT *View of the Creation maze at Varmlands in Sweden. The different elements of the design can be quite clearly discerned.*

Increasingly, the maze as an art-form is being sought for a wide range of contemporary applications. A hands-on science museum uses mazes to get visitors to think in non-verbal and non-numeric ways. A Christian minister has created a turf labyrinth within the grounds of a rehabilitation community. In a shopping precinct, a brick pavement maze provides an oasis of activity, as well as a decorative paving feature.

One clue to the enigma of the maze has been present throughout in our subconscious. The unconscious is often symbolised by corridors, passages, cellars, chambers, unlocked exits, labyrinths and mazes. An Egyptian papyrus of 1400 BC has been found portraying the seven doors of the Egyptian underworld, itself seen as a maze – a further link with the sevenfold nature of siege legends and the Classical labyrinth design.

The labyrinth of the subconscious becomes a visit to the underworld, literally another world, where everything familiar is replaced by a strange new logic. Distortions experienced in dreams have their parallel in the restricted paths and choices which mazes impose.

Jung maintained that in all cultures, the labyrinth has the meaning of an entangled and confusing representation of the world of matriarchal consciousness; it can be traversed only by those who are ready for a special initiation into the mysterious world of the collective unconscious. Within this interpretation, the Minotaur symbolises the decadence of matriarchal Crete,

with Theseus representing the young patriarchal spirit of Athens. His rescue of Ariadne denotes the liberation of the animal figure from the devouring aspect of the mother image, thus reaching his first true capacity for relations with women. The hero-monster battle is therefore a symbolic expression of growing up, and of breaking free from the psychic energy attached to the mother-son relationship, and becoming ready to achieve a more adult relationship with women. If this interpretation of the mass experience is expanded to act as a universal metaphor for coming of age for both men and women then the ubiquity and longevity of the maze begins to be explained. But perhaps the final riddle of the maze is not that it has proved so ubiquitous, but rather that mankind, driven by its need to create labyrinths for so many purposes, independently developed virtually the same Classical labyrinth design in different parts of the world, and then adhered to it for so many centuries.

Modern silver jewellery from Arizona, portraying the Man in the Maze. Modern methods and craftsmanship sustain the traditional labyrinth story in new forms of art, as well as in ancient rock carvings.

The classical labyrinth design is laid out on the beach at Point Reyes, California, to celebrate the Winter Solstice. This image captures the spirit of one of mankind's oldest forms, laid out by the present generation on the ground of the New World, overlooking the ocean of the future.

Gazetteer

The following Gazetteer lists selected mazes around the world by name, location, material, shape, size, designer(s) and date of opening. Roman Mosaic and Christian labyrinths are listed separately in tables in the text.

For the record:

LARGEST

World's largest hedge maze: Longleat Maze, Longleat House

World's largest symbolic hedge maze: Marlborough Maze, Blenheim Palace

World's largest brick pavement maze: Tudor Rose Maze, Kentwell Hall

World's largest turf maze: Saffron Walden Common

EARLIEST AND OLDEST

Earliest dateable labyrinth: either on Pylos tablet, Greece, *c.* 1200 BC, or on ceramic vessel found at Tell Rifa'at, Syria, *c.* 1300 BC

Earliest labyrinth coins: Knossos, Crete, 430 BC

Earliest Roman mosaic labyrinth: Rome, Italy, *c.* 100–80 BC

Earliest dateable labyrinth in the British Isles: Hollywood Stone, Ireland, *c.* 550 AD

Earliest dateable labyrinth in Scandinavia: 'Rosaring', Lassa, Uppland, Sweden, *c.* 815 AD

Earliest surviving medieval Christian labyrinth: Chartres Cathedral, France, 1235 AD

Britain's oldest surviving hedge maze: Hampton Court maze, 1690

Australia

A MAZE 'N THINGS, Grubb Road, Drysdale, Victoria, Australia; wooden maze with bridges

ASHCOMBE MAZE, Red Hill Road, Shoreham, Victoria, Australia; hedge maze

BELAIR MAZE, Belair Park, Adelaide, South Australia; circular hedge maze, 131 × 131 ft; 1890 (copy of maze in Forest of Dean)

BUNYA PARK MAZE, Eatons Hill, Brisbane, Queensland, Australia; wooden maze

CASTLE MAZE, Mittagong, New South Wales, Australia; wooden maze, with corner towers and wooden bridges; built 1980s

CRACKEN-BACK FARM, Jindabyne, New South Wales, Australia; wooden maze, 180 × 120 ft; designed by Stuart Landsborough, 1982

DUNTROON MAZE, Royal Military College, Duntroon, Canberra, ACT; yew hedges, planted 1962; copy of Hampton Court maze

FAUNA PARK MAZE, Fauna Park, Brisbane, Queensland, Australia; wooden maze

KRYAL CASTLE MAZE, Ballarat Highway, Ballarat, Victoria, Australia; brick walls maze

MARINO ROCKS MAZE, Marino Rocks, South Australia; teatree hedges; exact replica of Hampton Court maze; 1962

MURRAY BRIDGE MAZE, Murray Bridge, South Australia; wooden maze

RICHMOND MAZE, 13 Bridge Street, Richmond, Tasmania, Australia; hedges; built by Mike Hitchcock, 1980s.

SEQUOIA PARK MAZE, Sequoia Park, Neaves Road, Bullsbrook, Western Australia; wooden maze

SYDNEY MAZE, Sydney, NSW; pine log walls; built by Peter Batum, 1980s

WADONGA MAZE, Wadonga, Victoria, Australia; wooden maze

WESTON PARK MAZE, Weston Park, Canberra, ACT; pine log walls; built by Peter Batum, 1980s

Belgium

ADINKERKE MAZE, Avenue de la Panne, 82, Adinkerke, Belgium; Ligustrum hedges; rectangular, 158 × 158 ft; designed by M. A-J Florizoone, 1935

ENGHIEN MAZE, Château Enghein, Belgium; hedge maze; existed in 1922 (present condition not known)

GHENT MAZE, Great Hall, Ghent, Belgium; white and blue stone; design similar to St Omer; built by Walter van Werveke, 1533

HERCKENRODE MAZE, Herckenrode Abbey, Curange, Belgium; hedge maze; 56 × 46 ft; Cistercian nunnery

LOPPEM MAZE, Château de Loppem, near Bruges, Belgium; hedge 'dedale' with central tree; designed by Baron Charles de Caloen, 1859

MUSEUM VAN BUUREN MAZE, Brussels, Belgium; hedge maze

PYRAMID MAZE, Château de Beloeil, Belgium; beech hedges; 190 × 120 ft; designed by Randoll Coate, 1977

Bermuda

Pembroke Parish, Hamilton, Bermuda; bigonia hedge maze, planted early nineteenth century; inspired by Hampton Court maze

British Hedge Mazes

ALICE-IN-WONDERLAND MAZE, Merritown House, Dorset, England; octagonal, 240 × 240 ft; designed by Randoll Coate and Adrian Fisher, 1992

BLACKGANG CHINE MAZE, Blackgang Chine, Isle of Wight, England; privet hedges, rectangular, 84 × 75 ft; 1962

BLACKPOOL PLEASURE BEACH MAZE, Blackpool Pleasure Beach, Lancashire, England; privet hedges, rectangular, 125 × 90 ft; built 1937; based on Hampton Court design

BRIDGE END GARDENS MAZE, Saffron Walden, Essex, England; yew hedges, 160 × 70 ft; originally planted 1839, restored by John Bosworth, 1984

BRITANNIA MAZE, Wolseley Garden Park, Rugeley, Staffordshire, England; hedges, in shape of Britannia, 400 × 200 ft; designed by Lesley Beck and Adrian Fisher, 1991

CASTLE BROMWICH HALL GARDENS MAZE, Castle Bromwich Hall Gardens, West Midlands, England; holly and hawthorn hedges, rectangular mirror image of Hampton Court design, 76 × 23 ft; probably built by Lady Ida Bridgeman in late nineteenth century; restored by Martin Locock, 1990

CAWDOR MAZE, Cawdor Castle, Nairnshire, Scotland (O.S. Ref. NH 847498); square hedge maze; planted 1981

CRYSTAL PALACE MAZE, Crystal Palace, South London; hornbeam hedge maze, circular, 160 × 160 ft; planted *c.* 1865, restored by Patrick Phillips, 1988

DART VALLEY RAILWAY MAZE, Dart Valley Railway, Buckfastleigh, Devon, England; Cupressus leylandii hedges, rectangular; 1986

DRAGON MAZE, Newquay Zoo, Newquay, Cornwall, England; Eleagnus hedges, dragon-shaped, 210 × 85 ft; designed by Randoll Coate and Adrian Fisher, 1984

ENVIRONMENTAL MAZE, National Centre for Alternative Technology, Llwyngwern Quarry, Machynlleth, Powys, Wales; rhododendron, birch and oak hedges; designed by Pat Borer, 1980

ESPLANADE MAZE, The Esplanade, Scarborough, North Yorkshire, England; privet hedges, rectangular, 105 × 72 ft; 1963

GLENDURGAN MAZE, Glendurgan House, near Falmouth, Cornwall, England; laurel hedges, 133 × 108 ft; designed by Alfred Fox, 1833

HAMPTON COURT MAZE, Hampton Court Palace, East Molesey, Surrey, England; yew hedges, trapezoid, 222 × 82 ft; designed by George London and Henry Wise, 1690

HATFIELD BOX MAZE, Hatfield House, Herts, England; low box with gravel paths, square, 31 × 31 ft; in front of Old Palace, to be observed only, not walked in; designed by Lady Salisbury, 1980s.

HAZLEHEAD MAZE, Hazlehead Park, Aberdeen, Scotland; privet hedges, rectangular, 135 × 100 ft; built by Sir Henry Alexander, 1935

HEVER MAZE, Hever Castle, Edenbridge, Kent, England; yew hedges, square, 75 × 75 ft; built by William Waldorf Astor, 1905

ITALIANATE MAZE, Capel Manor, Bullsmoor Lane, Enfield, Middlesex, England; holly hedges, 121 × 88 ft; designed by Adrian Fisher, 1991

JUBILEE MAZE, Symonds Yat West, Nr Ross-on-Wye, Here & Worcs, England; Lawson's cypress hedges, octagonal, 135 × 135 ft; designed by Lindsay and Edward Heyes, 1981; also Maze Museum

LEEDS CASTLE MAZE, Maidstone, Kent, England; yew hedges and underground exit tunnel, square, 156 × 156 ft; designed by Randoll Coate, Adrian Fisher and Vernon Gibberd, 1988

LONGLEAT MAZE, Longleat House, near Warminster, Wiltshire, England; yew hedges and wooden bridges, rectangular, 380 × 175 ft; world's largest hedge maze; designed by Greg Bright, 1978

MARGAM MAZE, Margam Country Park, Port Talbot, West Glamorgan, Wales; Cupressus leylandii hedges, rectangular, 198 × 189 ft; built by Dr Terence Stevens, 1986

MARLBOROUGH MAZE, Blenheim Palace, Woodstock, Oxfordshire, England; yew hedges, 294 × 185 ft, rectangular; designed by Randoll Coate and Adrian Fisher, 1991

MISTLEY MAZE, Mistley Place, Manningtree, Essex, England; beech hedges, planted *c.* 1870; replanted in holly by Frank Pearson, 1989

RHINEFIELD MAZE, Rhinefield House, Hants, England; yew hedges, rectangular, 135 × 69 ft; based on Hampton Court design; built 1890, restored by Kim Wilkie, 1990

SALTWELL PARK MAZE, Saltwell Park, Gateshead, Tyne & Wear, England; rectangular, 86 × 46 ft; originally planted in yew hedges by William Wailes *c.* 1860; replanted in beech hedges, and was in poor condition by the 1970's; replanted with yew hedges, 1983

SOMERLEYTON MAZE, Somerleyton Hall, near Lowestoft, Suffolk, England; yew hedges, 245 × 160 ft; central pagoda; designed by William Nesfield, 1846

SPRINGFIELD MAZE, Springfield Gardens, Spalding, Lincolnshire; Cupressus leylandii Hedges, 75 × 75 ft; designed by Peter Atkinson, 1977

TATTON MAZE, Tatton Park, Knutsford, Cheshire, England; beech hedges, rectangular, 114 × 60 ft; copy of Hampton Court maze, planted *c.* 1890

TRAQUAIR MAZE, Traquair House, Peebles-shire, Scotland; Cupressus leylandii hedges, square, 147 × 147 ft; designed by John Schofield, 1980

VICTORIA PARK MAZE, Victoria Park, Scarborough, North Yorkshire, England; privet hedges, rectangular, 135 × 100 ft; 1959

WONDERLAND MAZE, Telford Town Park, Telford, Salop, England; beech hedges; 1989

WORDEN MAZE, Worden Park, Leyland, Lancashire, England; beech hedges, same design as Somerleyton Maze; designed by William Nesfield, 1886

British Turf Mazes

ARCHBISHOP'S MAZE, Greys Court, Henley-on-Thames, Oxfordshire, England (O.S. Ref. SU 725834); brick paths in grass, circular, 85 × 85 ft; designed by Randoll Coate and Adrian Fisher, 1981

BATH FESTIVAL MAZE, Beazer Gardens, nr Pulteney Bridge, Bath, Avon, England (O.S. Ref. ST 753649); Bath stone paths in grass, elliptical, 97 × 73 ft; mosaic centrepiece, 15 ft diameter; designed by Randoll Coate and Adrian Fisher, 1984

CHENIES MAZE, Chenies Manor House, Chenies, Buckinghamshire, England; gravel paths in grass, circular, 48 × 48 ft; design based on painting dated 1573 now hanging in Woburn Abbey; built by Denys Tweddell, 1983

CITY OF TROY, Dalby, North Yorkshire, England (O.S. Ref. SE 625719), near village of Brandsby; turf path, circular, 26 × 22 ft; seven-ring Classical design; beside road, enclosed by low white fencing

DODDINGTON MAZE, Doddington Hall, Doddington, Lincolnshire, England (O.S. Ref. SK 900697); gravel paths in grass, circular, 75 × 75 ft; designed by Mr Jarvis, 1985

GREAT BRITISH MAZE, Breamore Countryside Museum, Breamore, Hants, England; brick paths in grass, square, 52 × 52 ft; winner of *Sunday Times* maze design competition; designed by Ian Leitch, 1984

HILTON MAZE, The Common, Hilton, Cambridgeshire, England (O.S. Ref. TL 293663); turf path, circular, 55 × 55 ft; Medieval Christian design; central stone pillar dated 1660

JULIAN'S BOWER, Alkborough, South Humberside, England (O.S. Ref. SE 880218); turf paths, circular, 44 × 44 ft; Medieval Christian design, built certainly before 1671

LAPPA MAZE, Lappa Valley Railway, St Newlyn East, Cornwall, England; brick paths in grass, in shape of steam engine, 161 × 101 ft; designed by Randoll Coate and Adrian Fisher, 1982

LEIGHTON MAZE, Leighton Hall, Carnforth, Lancashire, England; gravel paths; 1990

MIZ-MAZE, Breamore Down, Breamore, Hampshire, England (O.S. Ref. SU 142203); turf maze, circular, 87 × 87 ft; Medieval Christian design

MIZ-MAZE, St Catherine's Hill, nr Winchester, Hants, England (O.S. Ref. SU 484278); turf maze, square, 96 × 96 ft; based on Medieval Christian design

PENNARD MAZE, Three Cliffs Bay, Pennard, Gower Peninsula, West Glamorgan (O.S. Ref. SS 539882); stone-lined paths in grass, circular, 30 × 30 ft; built by Jeff Saward, 1972

ROCKET MAZE, Springfield Park, Forest Hall, Nr Whitley Bay, North Yorkshire, England; gravel paths in grass, in shape of steam engine, 100 ft long; 1984

ROSE HILL QUARRY LABYRINTH, Rose Hill Quarry, Swansea, West Glamorgan (O.S. Ref. SS 644935); gravel paths in turf, circular, 30 × 30 ft; seven-ring Classical design, built by Bob Shaw, 1987

SAFFRON WALDEN TURF MAZE, The Common, Saffron Walden, Essex (O.S. Ref. TL 543385); brick paths in turf, circular with bastions, 132 × 132 ft; seventeen rings, Medieval Christian design

TROY TOWN, St Agnes, Scilly Isles (O.S. Refs. SV 876078 and SV 878078); several stone-lined path labyrinths in grass, circular, various sizes

TROY TOWN, St Martins, Scilly Isles (O.S. Ref. SV 923170); several stone-lined path labyrinths in grass, circular, various sizes

WARRINGTON TURF MAZE, Parkfield, Warrington, Cheshire, England (O.S. Ref. SJ 630914); gravel paths in grass, circular, 60 × 60 ft; 1985

WILLEN MAZE, Willen Lake, Milton Keynes, Buckinghamshire, England (O.S. Ref. SP 880405); gravel paths in grass, circular with bastions, 345 × 345 ft; enlarged copy of Saffron Walden; built 1984

WING MAZE, The Common, Wing, Leicestershire, England (O.S. Ref. SK 895028); turf paths, circular, 50 × 50 ft; Medieval Christian design

Other British Mazes

ALKBOROUGH CHURCH, Alkborough, South Humberside (O.S. Ref. SE 882219); stained-glass window; nineteenth century

ALKBOROUGH CHURCH PORCH, Alkborough, South Humberside, England (O.S. Ref. SE 882219); stone pavement maze, circular, 6 × 6 ft; 1887

APOTHECARIES WINDOW MAZE, Apothecaries Hall, Blackfriars Lane, City of London; College of Arms, maze design by Adrian Fisher, 1989 (not open to the public)

BATHEASTON CHURCH, Batheaston, Avon, England (O.S. Ref. ST 777679); stone pavement, square, 16 × 16 ft; built by Rev Paul Lucas, 1985

BICTON MAZE, Bicton Park, Devon, England; upright wooden logs, in shape of footprint, 160 × 75 ft; designed by Randoll Coate and Adrian Fisher, 1986

BOURN CHURCH, Bourn, Cambridgeshire, England (O.S. Ref. TL 325563); black and red tiles, rectangular, 15 × 12 ft; design based on Hampton Court maze; built 1875

BRISTOL WATER MAZE, Victoria Park, Bristol, Avon, England (O.S. Ref. ST 595716); water maze in brick channel, circular, 20 × 20 ft; designed by Peter Milner and Jane Norbury, 1984

ELY MAZE, Ely Cathedral, Ely, Cambridgeshire, England (O.S. Ref. TL 541803); black and white stone pavement maze, square, 20 × 20 ft; designed by Sir Gilbert Scott, 1870

HULL MAZE, King Edward St, Hull, North Humberside, England; brick pavement, square, 43 × 43 ft; built by Philip Heselton, 1987

IRVINE TOWN CENTRE, Irvine New Town, Ayrshire, Scotland; stained glass window, circular, 5 × 5 ft; 1980s

IRVINE BEACH MAZE, Irvine Beach Park, Irvine New Town, Ayrshire, Scotland; concrete paths in grass, circular, 108 × 108 ft; 1980s

LANDMARK MAZE, Landmark Centre, Nr Carrbridge, Scotland; raised wooden paths in woodland; *c.* 1978

LION RAMPANT MAZE, Worksop Town Centre, Nottinghamshire, England; brick pavement; rectangular, 45 × 33 ft; designed by Lesley Beck, Randoll Coate and Adrian Fisher, 1989

MAPPA MUNDI, Hereford Cathedral, England

(O.S. Ref. SO 510398); shows medieval Christian labyrinth on island of Crete; completed by Richard de Bello *c.* 1280 AD, brought to Hereford in 1305

MAYFLOWER MAZE, Mayflower Park, Southampton, Hampshire, England; low concrete walls, hexagonal; 1980s

MAZE OF THE MYSTERIES OF THE GOSPELS, Wyck Rissington Church, Gloucestershire, England; wall mosaic; 3 × 2 ft; based on hedge maze design by Canon Harry Cheales; mosaic design by Adrian Fisher, 1988

ROCKY VALLEY CARVINGS, Rocky Valley, Tintagel, Cornwall, England (OS Ref. SX 073894); two rock carvings, circular; 9 × 9ins, and 9 × 7 ins

SNAKES AND LADDERS MAZE, Ragley Hall, Alcester, Warwickshire, England; tall concrete walls, on two levels, rectangular; originally built by Maurice Rich, *c.* 1980

ST MARY REDCLIFFE MAZE, St Mary Redcliffe Church, Bristol, Avon, England (O.S. Ref. ST 591723); carved and gilded wooden roof boss in north aisle; eleven-ring Medieval Christian design, circular, 8 × 8 ins; fifteenth century

TEMPLE NEWSAM MAZE, Temple Newsam House, Leeds, West Yorkshire, England; brick paths in gravel, rectangular, 114 × 92 ft; built 1976

TUDOR ROSE MAZE, Kentwell Hall, Long Melford, Suffolk, England (O.S. Ref. TL 863479); brick pavement, 80 × 70 ft; designed by Randoll Coate and Adrian Fisher, 1985

UNICORN RAMPANT MAZE, Worksop Town Centre, Nottinghamshire, England; brick pavement; rectangular, 39 × 27 ft; designed by Lesley Beck, Randoll Coate and Adrian Fisher, 1990

WARREN STREET MAZE, Warren Street, London WC1, England; brick pavement maze, square; designed by John Burrell, 1979

WATTS MEMORIAL CHAPEL, Compton, Surrey (O.S. Ref. SU 956474); corbels of four angels holding labyrinths, and a fifth labyrinth incorporated within altar; built 1896

YORK GATE MAZE, York Gate, Adel, Leeds, West Yorkshire, England; granite setts in gravel, circular, 21 × 21 ft; built by Mrs Sybil Spencer, 1979

Canada

TREE TOPS MAZE, Tree Tops, Carleton, Yarmouth County, Nova Scotia; hedge maze, 168 × 136 ft; built by Robert K Allen, 1976

VANDUSEN GARDENS MAZE, Vandusen Gardens, Vancouver, British Columbia; hedge maze

Denmark

There have been many dozens of turf mazes in Denmark, mostly named Trojborg or Trelleborg, but none have survived to the present day. Existing mazes in Denmark include:

EGESKOV MAZE, Egeskov on Fyn Island, Denmark; rectangular hedge maze.

GEVNINGE CHURCH, Denmark; wall-paintings of two eleven-ring Classical labyrinths, *c.* fifteenth century

HESSELAGER CHURCH, Denmark; wall-painting of eleven-ring Classical labyrinth, *c.* fifteenth century

SKIVE OLD CHURCH, Denmark; wall-painting of fifteen-ring Classical labyrinth, *c.* fifteenth century

TROJBORG, Gerlev, Denmark; stone-lined paths, Classical labyrinth design; built 1985

TROJBORG, Lejre, Denmark; stone-lined paths, Classical labyrinth design; built 1979

TROJBORG, Nonshoved, Denmark; stone-lined paths, Classical labyrinth design; built after 1985

TROJBORG, Tulstrup, Denmark; stone-lined paths, Classical labyrinth design; built 1976

Finland

There are over one hundred and fifty stone-lined path labyrinths in Finland. Existing labyrinths in Finland include:

SIBBO CHURCH, Finland; wall painting (depicting female figure standing at the centre of an eleven-ring Classical labyrinth); fifteenth century

KANTMAKI CHURCH, Finland; stone-lined paths; eleven-ring Classical labyrinth

Island near Borgo, Finland; stone-lined paths; fifteen-ring Processional labyrinth

France

Listed separately: Roman Mosaic labyrinths: Chusclan, Gard, Lyons (2), Nîmes, Pont-Chevron, Verdes; medieval Christian pavement labyrinths: Amiens, Bayeux, Chartres, Genainville, Mirepoix, Orleans, St Quentin, Toulouse; later Church mazes: Guingamp, Mailly-Maillet, Selestat.

CHATEAU DE BALLEUIL, France; hedge maze; designed by M. Motzler, planted 1989

CHATEAU DE LA BATISSE, Chanonet, Puy-de-Dome, France; puzzle hedge maze, built eighteenth century

CHATEAU DE BEAUMESNIL, Beaumesnil, Normandy, France; maze on ruin of a dungeon, on a small lake

CHATEAU DE BRETEUIL, Breteuil, Ile-de-France; hedge maze; rectangular

LA GAUDE, Aix-en-Provence, France; block-type labyrinthine pattern, though not a true puzzle maze; on island in front of château

LA COMMANDERIE DE NEUILLY, Neuilly-sous-Clermont, Oise, France; hornbeam hedges; circular, 39 × 39 ft; built by Jean Aries, 1988

JARDIN DES PLANTES, Paris, France; hedge maze originally built in eighteenth century, with central summerhouse and pendulum bell; hedge maze with statue of St John Perse, restored 1990

CHATEAU DE PONCE, Ponce, Loire, France; hornbeam hedges, rectangular; one entrance at each of four corners

RENNES, France; hedge maze; built by Madame Arthaud

CHATEAUNEUF LE ROUGE, Aix en Provence, France; hedge maze, 300 years old?

CHATEAU DE VILLANDRY, Indre-et-Loire, France; hornbeam hedges, in poor condition; 131 × 89 ft

LE LABYRINTHE AUX OISEAUX, Château d'Yvoire, Yvoire, Douvaine, Haute-Savoie, France; within Le Jardin de Cinq Sens; built by Mme Anne-Monique d'Yvoire, 1989

Germany

BAD WALDLIESBORN, near Lippstadt, West Germany; woodland maze with meandering pathways, with central millstone on pedestal

BAD WALDLIESBORN, near Lippstadt, West

Germany; beech hedge maze; circular, 60 × 60 ft

BAD WALDLIESBORN, near Lippstadt, West Germany; paving slabs in grass; seven-ring Classical design; square, 50 × 50 ft

HERRENHAUSEN GARDENS, Hannover, West Germany; hedge maze with central octagonal pavilion; octagonal, 76 × 76 ft; probably built by Michael Grosse, 1674; restored 1936

COLOGNE CATHEDRAL, Cologne, West Germany; black and white marble labyrinth, octagonal, $4\frac{1}{2} \times 4\frac{1}{2}$ ft; designed by Dr Arnold Wolff, 1977

THE RAD, Eilenreide Forest, Hannover, West Germany; nine-ring Processional turf labyrinth, circular, 105 × 105 ft; has existed since at least 1642

SCHWEDENRING, Steigra, East Germany; eleven-ring Classical turf labyrinth, oval, 40 × 36 ft

SCHWEDENHIEB OF SCHWEDENSCHANZE, Graitchen, nr Camburg, East Germany; eleven-ring Classical turf labyrinth, circular, 32 × 32 ft

TREVES CATHEDRAL, Rhenanie-Palatinate, West Germany; blue stone eight-ring labyrinth with rose at centre; circular, 20 × 20 ins

TROJABURG, Folk Museum, Bunde, West Germany; stone lined paths, eleven-ring Classical labyrinth; circular, 29.5 × 29.5 ft; built by Professor Friedrich Langewiesche, 1940

Holland

GUNTERSTEIN MAZE, Gunterstein, Holland; hedge maze

KASTEEL WELDAM MAZE, Goor, Holland; hedge maze

MENKEMABORG UITHUIZEN, Groningen, Holland; rectangular hedge maze

GROETEN VAN DE BRAAK DOOLHOF, Paterswolde, Groningen Province, Holland; circular hedge maze with tree at centre; early 1900s

WILLOW MAZE, University of Technology, Eindhoven, Holland; willow hedges; eleven-ring Medieval Christian design; circular, 76 × 76 ft; built by Professor Peter Schmid, 1984

India

TEMPLE OF HOYSALESVARA, Halebid, Mysore, India; seven-ring Classical labyrinth, circular, 12 × 10 ins; *c.* 1100–1300 AD

TEMPLE OF KEDARESVARA, Halebid, Mysore, India; seven-ring Classical labyrinth, circular, 6 × 6 ins; *c.* 1100–1300 AD

Republic of Ireland

BURT, Church of St Regnus, Burt, Co. Donegal, Eire; (Map Ref. C 365212); church decorated with many seven-ring Classical labyrinths, with central Christian crosses; consecrated in 1967

HOLLYWOOD STONE, National Museum, Kildare St, Dublin, Eire; stone carved with seven-ring Classical labyrinth; 4 × 3 ft; *c.* 550 AD

RATHMORE, Co. Meath, Eire; in St Lawrence's Church; Medieval Christian labyrinth design, carved in stone; circular, 14 × 14 ins; mid-fifteenth century

RUSSBOROUGH MAZE, Russborough, Blessington, Co. Wicklow, Eire; beech hedge maze, with central statue on pillar; square, 142 × 142 ft; designed by Randoll Coate and Adrian Fisher, 1993

Italy

Listed separately: Classical labyrinths: Luzzanas, Val Camonica, Tragliatella Vase; Roman Mosaic labyrinths: Brindisi, Piadena, Cremona, Giannutri, Nora, Ostia, Pompeii (4), Rome (3), Selinunte, Syracuse; medieval Christian pavement labyrinths: Lucca, Ravenna, Rome.

VILLA BARBARIGO, Vansanzibio, Venice, Italy; hedge maze with small tower at centre; 230 × 230 ft; built 1669/1688

VILLA PISANI, Stra, nr Padua, Italy; hedge maze; central tower with twin staircases and statue of Minerva; built 1720

VILLA GARZONI, Collodi, Tuscany, Italy; square hedge maze

PALACE GIUSTI, Verona, Lombardia, Italy; rectangular hedge maze with fountain at centre

DONNA FUGATA, Sicily, Italy; hedge maze

Japan

There are over 150 wooden fence mazes in Japan, all built since 1984, of which 20 were designed by Stuart Landsborough:

AKIYOSHIDAI, Yamaguchi-Ken Mine-Gun Bito-Cho, Shimizu 1212; wooden maze; designed by Stuart Landsborough

DAIGO GRAN MAZE, Kyoto-Shi Fushimi-Ku Momoyama-Cho, Yamanoshita 19–6; wooden maze; designed by Stuart Landsborough

HAKODATE, Hokkaido Kayabe-Gun Mori-Machi, Komagadake 515–11; wooden maze; designed by Stuart Landsborough

HAZAKI, Ibaragi-Ken Kashima-Gun Hazaki-Cho, Yakabe Tuchigou 8762–13; wooden maze; designed by Stuart Landsborough

HIKIMI, Shimane-Ken Mino-Gun Hikimi-Cho, Hikimi; wooden maze; designed by Stuart Landsborough

KAGOSHIMA, Kagoshima-Shi Yojirou 1–7–15; wooden maze; designed by Stuart Landsborough

KISO, Nagano-Ken Kiso-Gun Kisomura,Kodamanomori; wooden maze; designed by Stuart Landsborough

KOBE, Kobe-Shi Tarumi-Ku Higashitarumi, Takamaru 762–11; wooden maze; designed by Stuart Landsborough

KOSUGI, Toyama-Ken Imizu-Gun Kosugi-Cho, Sanke 2602; wooden maze; designed by Stuart Landsborough

LALAPORT, Funabashi-Shi Hama-Machi 2–3–1; wooden maze; designed by Stuart Landsborough

MIHO, Shizuoka-Ken Shimizu-Shi Miho 238; wooden maze; designed by Stuart Landsborough

MIROKUNO-SATO, Hiroshima-Ken Numakuma-Gun Numakuma-Cho, Yamanaka; wooden maze; designed by Stuart Landsborough

MISASA, Tottori-Ken Tohaku-Gun Misasa-Cho, Misasakogen; wooden maze; designed by Stuart Landsborough

MITO, Mito-Shi Kobuki-Machi, Arayama 2701; wooden maze; designed by Stuart Landsborough

RITTO, Shiga-Ken Kurita-Gun Ritto-Cho, Ono 83–2; wooden maze; designed by Stuart Landsborough

SENMAN, Osaka-Fu Sennan-Shi Kitano 260; wooden maze; designed by Stuart Landsborough

SHIMOTU, Wakayama-Ken, Kaiso-Gun Shimotu-Cho, Kami 318–1; wooden maze; designed by Stuart Landsborough

TAKASAKI, Takasaki-Shi Kuragano-Cho 4711; wooden maze; designed by Stuart Landsborough

YOKKAICHI, Yokkaichi-Shi Tameru Koyanagi-Cho 2–11; wooden maze; designed by Stuart Landsborough

YOKOHAMA, Yokohama-Shi Kohoku-Ku, Eda-Cho 5265–1; wooden maze; designed by Stuart Landsborough

New Zealand

CAROLYNE BAY, Timaru, New Zealand; one level wooden maze, early 1980s

QUEEN ELIZABETH 2ND PARK, Christchurch, New Zealand; large wooden maze with one bridge level; copy of Wanaka maze; built early 1980s

RAINBOWSEND MAZE, Rainbowsend Entertainment Park, Manakau City, Auckland, New Zealand; four levels high wooden maze, 150 × 120 ft; designed by Stuart Landsborough, 1983

ROTORUA HEDGE MAZE, Rotorua, North Island, New Zealand; circular hedge maze; planted *c.* 1980

ROTORUA WOODEN MAZE, Rotorua, North Island, New Zealand; wooden maze with one bridge level; copy of Wanaka maze; built 1983

WANAKA MAZE, Wanaka, South Island, New Zealand; wooden maze with bridges; designed by Stuart Landsborough, 1973

WANGAREI MAZE, Wangarei, New Zealand; community project; hedge maze

WHANGANUI MAZE, Whanganui, New Zealand; small wooden maze, built early 1980s

Norway

There are over twenty stone-lined labyrinths in Norway, including:

DEN JULIANSKE BORG, Myklebust Farm, Mountain of Grothorn, Orsta, Sunnmore Province, Norway; 3,300 ft above sea level Vartdals Mountain, Orsta, Sunnmore Province, Norway; 3,000 ft above sea level

Poland

WINDELBAHN ('coil-track'), Stolp, Pomerania, Poland; turf labyrinth, with Processional path; used by the Shoemaker's Guild; original labyrinth destroyed. Copy made in 1935, present condition not known

Portugal

CONIMBRIGA, Coimbre, Portugal; black and white Roman mosaic, built *c.* 150–250 AD, discovered 1899; now in Machado de Castro Museum

Soviet Union

There are over sixty stone-lined path labyrinths in the Soviet Union, including:

GREAT HARE ISLAND, Solovecke, USSR; Processional labyrinth

WEIR ISLAND, Gulf of Finland, Soviet Union (formerly in Finland); stone-lined paths; unusual spiral labyrinth

South Africa

PIETERMARITZBURG CATHEDRAL, Natal, South Africa; pavement labyrinth, built 1981; copy of pavement maze in Ely Cathedral, England

Spain

BARCELONA, Spain; in the gardens of the Marquis of Alfarras; hedge maze with arboreal arches, statues and fountains; built 1922

LA GRANJA, Castilla La Vieja, near Segovia, Spain; in the Royal Gardens

MUSEUM OF NAVARRE, Pamplona, Spain; Roman mosaic labyrinth

Sri Lanka

Temple with seven-ring Classical fresco labyrinth; circular; 1755

Sweden

There are over three hundred stone-lined path labyrinths in Sweden. Existing labyrinths and mazes include:

AXELON, Varmland, Sweden; four preserved labyrinths on island in Lake Vanern

'CREATION', Varmlands Saby, Varmlands Province, Sweden; Amelanchier hedge maze; egg-shaped, 165 × 132 ft; designed by Randoll Coate, built 1979, opened 1985

FROJEL LABYRINTH, Island of Gotland, Sweden; located in the present churchyard, 40 ft east of the church, though once the churchyard was smaller. Stone-lined paths; seven-ring Classical labyrinth, excellently restored in 1974. The fourteenth century spelling Froale and Froyiale combines the fertility goddess Freja, and 'Al' meaning sanctuary.

GANGBORG, Lindbacke, Sweden; stone-lined paths; seven-ring Classical labyrinth

JUNGFRAU LABYRINTH, Jungfrau Island, Sweden; stone-lined paths, circular

KAROLINSKA SJUKHUSET HOSPITAL, Stockholm, Sweden; stone-lined path labyrinth, built in 1890s

KULERYD, Sweden; stone-lined paths; unusual coiled-path labyrinth

LINDBACKE, Nykoping, Sodermanland, Sweden; stone-lined paths; seven-ring Classical labyrinth; near ancient grave field with 45 graves, and close to a spring, belonging to the god Frej

REVONSAARI, North Sweden; stone-lined paths; seven-ring Classical labyrinth

'ROSARING', Lassa Socken, Uppland, Sweden; stone-lined paths; fifteen-ring Classical labyrinth; earliest dateable labyrinth in Scandinavia, *c.* 815 AD

STOREBERG, Gothenburg, Vastergotland, Sweden; stone-lined paths, seven-ring Classical labyrinth; re-discovered and restored by John Kraft and others in 1982

TRALLESTAD or TRELLEBOSTAN, Tvingelshed, Sweden; stone-lined paths; unusual coiled-path labyrinth

TRELLEBORG, Johanneshus, Parish of Vittaryd, Smaland, Sweden; stone-lined paths; seven-ring anticlockwise Classical labyrinth

TROJIENBORG, Tibble, Badelunde parish, Vastmansland, Sweden; stone-lined paths; fifteen-ring Classical labyrinth; named on local map of 1764 as Trojienborg

TROLLEBO STAD, Perstop, Sweden; stone-lined paths; seven-ring anticlockwise Classical labyrinth

VISBY LABYRINTH, Island of Gotland, Sweden; Sweden's most well-known labyrinth, immediately north of the old town of Visby; stone-lined paths, eleven-ring Classical labyrinth; earliest written record of this labyrinth is on a map of 1740; one of nearly forty labyrinths on the Island of Gotland

Switzerland

Listed separately: Roman Mosaic Labyrinths – Avrenches Museum, Baugy, Cormerod, Orbe.

MIRROR MAZE, Glacier Garden, Lucerne, Switzerland; walls of mirrors in 60° alignment

WALL MAZE, Ornamental plaque, Augustinergasse 6, Zurich, Switzerland; *c.* 1345; No. 4 is "Zum Irrgarten"

USA

AMHERST MAZE, University of Massachusetts, Amherst, Mass., USA; chain link fences; 61 × 61 ft; designed by Richard Fleischner, 1978

ARKVILLE CHRISTIAN MAZE (private), Dry Brook, Arkville, New York State, USA; cobbles and brick octagonal pavement; designed by Michael Ayrton, 1969

ARKVILLE MAZE (private), Dry Brook, Arkville, New York State, USA; tall brick walls; 200 ft across; designed by Michael Ayrton, 1969

'BIG THUNDER', Solar Oasis, Civic Plaza, Phoenix, Arizona; pavement colour maze with nine mosaics; 140 × 80 ft; designed by Lesley Beck and Adrian Fisher, 1992

CASA GRANDE MAZE, Casa Grande, Gila Valley, South Arizona, USA; 7-ring wall carving; 20″ diam; *c.* 1100–1200 AD

CEDAR HILLS MAZE (private), Cedar Hills, Waltham, Mass., USA; hedge maze, based on Hampton Court maze design, 1896; present condition unknown

DEERFIELD MAZE, Rydal, Pennsylvania, USA; 3 ft high boxwood hedges; squared copy of Hampton Court maze; created by Mr and Mrs Thomas Hallowell, Jr., in the 1940s

DOLPHINS MAZE, Poynter Park, St Petersburg, Florida, USA; paths in grass; 160 × 80 ft; designed by Lesley Beck and Adrian Fisher, 1992

GREENSBORO MAZE (private), Greensboro, Vermont, USA; circular 7-ring turf labyrinth; 24 ft diam.; built by Sig Lonegren, 1986

HEMET MAZE, 5 miles west of Hemet, California, USA; rock carving; date unknown

MAGIC HARBOR MAZE, Magic Harbor, Myrtle Beach, South Carolina, USA; privet hedges; 1983

NAVANO LABYRINTH, Navano, California, USA; turf labyrinth; built by Alex Champion, 1987

NEW HARMONY MAZE, New Harmony, Indiana, USA; privet hedges; circular, 140 × 140 ft; planted 1939 (adjacent to site of original vine hedge maze of 1814, which was destroyed in 1850)

NEWPORT MAZE, Chateau-Sur-Mer, Newport, Rhode Island, USA; designed by Richard Fleischner, 1980s

OJAI LABYRINTH, Ojai Community, Ojai, near Santa Barbara, California, USA; stone-lined paths, seven-ring Classical labyrinth; circular, 25 × 25 ft; built by Nigel Pennick, 1986

OMEGA MAZE, Omega Center, USA; stone-lined paths, seven-ring Classical labyrinth; circular; built by Paul Devereux, 1989

ORAIBI MAZE, Oraibi, Arizona, USA; rock carving, still in situ; seven-ring anticlockwise square Classical labyrinth; date unknown

OLD ORAIBI MAZE, now in Heard Museum, Phoenix, Arizona; stone-carved Labyrinth found at Old Oraibi; seven-ring square 'Mother and Child' labyrinth design; carved by Hopi indians; 1 × 1 ft (Heard Museum inventory NA–SW–HO–V–1)

POINT REYES LABYRINTHS, Point Reyes, California, USA; stone labyrinths, built by Chris Castle, 1980s

SHIPAULOVI MAZE CARVING, near pueblo of Hopi, North Arizona, USA; rock carving; date unknown

WILLIAMSBURG MAZE, The Governor's House, Williamsburg, Virginia, USA; holly hedges; 95 × 88 ft; based on Hampton Court maze design, built 1935

WOOZ MAZE, Vacaville, California, USA; wooden maze with bridges; built 1988

THE MAZES OF MINOTAUR DESIGNS

Opening dates are shown, not construction dates (mazes no longer existing are shown in brackets).

('EMBRYO'), Bournemouth, Dorset; private; 1975
'IMPRINT', Lechlade, Glos; private; 1975
'PYRAMID', Château de Beloeil, Belgium; 1977
'CREATION', Varmlands Saby, Sweden; 1979
ARCHBISHOP'S MAZE, Greys Court, Oxon; 1981
LAPPA MAZE, Lappa Valley Railway, Cornwall; 1982
(ROXBURGHE MAZE), Floors Castle, Scotland; 1983
DRAGON MAZE, Newquay Zoo, Cornwall; 1984
(MAGNETIC MAZE), Thorpe Park, Surrey; 1984
(BEATLES' MAZE), International Garden Festival '84 Liverpool; (1984 only)
BATH FESTIVAL MAZE, Beazer Gardens, Bath; 1984
TUDOR ROSE MAZE, Kentwell Hall, Suffolk; 1985
(BYGRAVE MAZE), St Alban's Herts; 1985
BICTON MAZE, Bicton Park, Devon; 1986
MAZE OF THE MYSTERIES OF THE GOSPELS, Wyck Rissington, Glos; wall mosaic; 1988
LEEDS CASTLE MAZE, Kent; 1988
APOTHECARIES' WINDOW MAZE, Apothecaries' Hall, London; Fisher, 1989
LION RAMPANT MAZE, Worksop, Notts; 1989
UNICORN RAMPANT MAZE, Worksop, Notts; 1990
(ROLAWN TURF MAZE), National Garden Festival '90, Gateshead; (1990 only)
GARDEN COLOUR MAZE, Surrey; private; 1990
MATHEMATICAL COLOUR MAZE, Leicester University; 1990
MARLBOROUGH MAZE, Blenheim Palace, Oxon; 1991
ITALIANATE MAZE, Capel Manor, Enfield, Middlesex; 1991
BRITANNIA MAZE, Wolseley Garden Park, Staffs; 1991
ALICE-IN-WONDERLAND MAZE, Merritown House, Dorset; 1992
'BIG THUNDER', Solar Oasis, Phoenix, Arizona; 1992
DOLPHINS MAZE, Poynter Park, St Petersburg, Florida; 1992
RUSSBOROUGH MAZE, Co. Wicklow, Eire; 1993

Further Reading

BORD, Janet, *Mazes and Labyrinths of the World* (Latimer, London, 1976). A good pictorial guide to mazes and labyrinths, especially in the UK. Now out of print.

BORGES, Jorge Luis, *Labyrinths* (Penguin Modern Classis, London, 1962). A remarkable collection of stories and essays set in a labyrinthine world. 'A wealth of invention and tight, almost mathematical, style'.

COATE, R., FISHER, A. and BURGESS, G., *A Celebration of Mazes*, 4th ed. (Minotaur Publications, St Alban's, 1986). A general history of the world's mazes, with symbolic mazes discussed in detail. Contains catalogue of mazes throughout the world open to the public. 80 pages, 59 illustrations.

KERN, Hermann, *Labyrinthe* (Prestel-Verlag, Munich, 1982). The most comprehensive reference material for labyrinths of all kinds, though little on modern mazes. German text, 491 pages, 666 illustrations.

KRAFT, John, *The Goddess in the Labyrinth* (Abo Akademi, 1985). A well-researched collection of labyrinth myths and legends. Also by John Kraft, over twenty other published works, mainly in Swedish, containing impressive and meticulous research, particularly on Scandinavian labyrinths.

MATTHEWS, W. H., *Mazes and Labyrinths – their history and development* (1922, reprinted by Dover, New York, 1970). Still the definitive work on mazes. Thoroughly researched, very readable, though inevitably deficient on twentieth-century mazes. 254 pages, 151 illustrations.

THE MAZE SOCIETY, Capel Manor, Bullsmoor Lane, Enfield, Middlesex, EN1 4RQ, England. Various publications.

PENNICK, Nigel, *Labyrinths, Their Geomancy and Symbolism* (Runestaff, Cambridge, 1984). Useful study of symbolism of the labyrinth. 40 page booklet.

SAINT-HILAIRE, Paul de, *Le Mystère des Labyrinthes* (Rossel, Brussels, 1977). A lively if uneven catalogue. In French.

SANTARCANGELI, Paulo, *Il libro dei labyrinti* (Vallecchi Editore, Firenze, 1967). Thought-provoking study of myths and traditions connected with the labyrinth symbol. 393 pages, 135 illustrations.

SAWARD, Jeff, (editor), *Caerdroia Magazine* (Caerdroia Publications, 53 Thundersley Grove, Thundersley, Benfleet, Essex, over 20 issues since 1980). The journals of the Caerdroia Project are a lively forum for the exchange of ideas, as well as collectively being excellent source material.

SAWARD, Jeff, *The Caerdroia Field Guide*, 1st ed. (Caerdroia Publications, Benfleet, 1987). Excellent guide to ancient and recent labyrinths throughout the UK.

Index

Numbers in **bold** denote illustrations.